HEAVEN KNOWS WHY

REAL ANGEL CONTACT PHOTOS AND TRUE PAST LIFE CONVERSATIONS

Christine Snowdon

BALBOA.
PRESS

A DIVISION OF HAY HOUSE

Balboa Press books may be ordered through booksellers or by contacting:

Balboa Press
A Division of Hay House
1663 Liberty Drive
Bloomington, IN 47403
www.balboapress.com
1 (877) 407-4847

Because of the dynamic nature of the Internet, any web addresses or links contained in this book may have changed since publication and may no longer be valid. The views expressed in this work are solely those of the author and do not necessarily reflect the views of the publisher, and the publisher hereby disclaims any responsibility for them.

The author of this book does not dispense medical advice or prescribe the use of any technique as a form of treatment for physical, emotional, or medical problems without the advice of a physician, either directly or indirectly. The intent of the author is only to offer information of a general nature to help you in your quest for emotional and spiritual well-being. In the event you use any of the information in this book for yourself, which is your constitutional right, the author and the publisher assume no responsibility for your actions.

Any people depicted in stock imagery provided by Thinkstock are models, and such images are being used for illustrative purposes only.
Certain stock imagery © Thinkstock.

Printed in the United States of America.

ISBN: 978-1-4525-2009-4 (sc)
ISBN: 978-1-4525-2011-7 (hc)
ISBN: 978-1-4525-2010-0 (e)

Library of Congress Control Number: 2014914465

Balboa Press rev. date: 10/15/2014

CONTENTS

I give gratitude to my family on earth and in spirit for your loving support. And to our family pet dog 'Joy' who passed to heaven recently after sharing many years of joy, fun and love with us

FOREWORD

God has a sense of humour. When the voice of the most powerful energy known to man, who is all-loving, all-caring, and all-knowing said clearly, "It is my second-dearest wish," I could almost hear him chuckle.

An angelic realm is a solar system where a collective of angels resides. Each realm comprises several angel groups, all of whom have specific essential functions to perform. There are over forty angel realms in our universe and over two hundred outside our universe.

God, as we like to call him or her, has all the human qualities that we have, as we were created out of this being's love, and love is all there is. Just like the song by the Beatles says, "All you need is love." I have learned through teaching of angelic Reiki and guidance that if you work through your heart, from the basis of love, all will come right and true. Put another way, as the saying goes, "All crooked roads will be straightened."

The movement of planets in our solar system affects our actions and responses; our lives are not predestined. We have a purpose in life and that purpose is discussed with us in the spirit world with us before we are born on earth.

My own journey in spirit has been guided by coloured visions that appear in mid-air in the middle of the night. I was not frightened when they appeared. I stared in awe at the first one, Archangel Michael, from whom I now channel messages regularly. I also channel messages from other archangels and masters. I know I am being guided by the angels to pass these communications on to help enlighten people and encourage world peace.

By writing these books I also hope to pass on spiritual information that anybody can understand and encourage you to become aware of angels, guides, ascended masters, and the colour rays and energies that they resonate with. This will, in turn, demonstrate that they can bring change to our lives for the highest good of everyone.

We can all learn from the higher attributes of each other's star signs and endeavour to aspire to them in addition to our own. For example, the earth, water, air, and fire star groups are easy to learn, and we should respect their different aspects.

At the end of each chapter is an affirmation for you to think about. Each one will help you understand a bit more about your higher self, which is always with you and can be tapped into at any time. Your connection with the angelic realm can start with a little prayer, a lighted candle, some gentle music, and a desire to know and be aware of the guardian angel who is with you all the time. Every single person on this planet has a guardian angel. If you ask for a sign, it will find a way. Maybe a feather will appear in front of you out of the blue, a song will be played every time you turn on the radio, or a name will appear with an angelic reference.

This is your guardian angel's way of showing you it is aware of your every thought, word, and deed, and that it loves you very much. Guardian angels resonate with love. Once you are aware of this, you can ask for their help with every struggle, achievement, wish, and dream in your life. I wish you happiness along the way.

May all your dreams of a golden future come true.

The Vision

With eyes half-open, I can see
A glowing angel close to me,
Turning into violet, and then
Knowing she'll return again.

***

Drifting off, my thoughts of pure
Dreams of futures to endure,
Before all knowledge comes to man.
Guardian angel, take my hand.

***

Against the night, I see your face,
Shining yellow, full of grace.
Your vision will remain with me.
In God's own time, the world will see.

CHAPTER 1

Spirit and Soul Energy

Every experience has been created by us so it is important to not feel guilty if we find ourselves in a bad situation. I had complained for nearly ten years about where I lived while being unable to move to a different area. It also added weight to the concept that sometimes if we want something too badly, we can drive it away from ourselves and continue along a path of not getting what we truly need.

Therefore, we need to look objectively at each situation to pursue our life's purpose at leisure. We do this while checking the signposts along the way and re-evaluating our lifestyle, career, and living accommodations from a soul's point of view. This puts us in a position to have a positive mind-set, which is the best way to move forward. It will set the universal wheels in motion instead of blocking our aspirations.

Does Mental Illness Cause Religious Experiences?

I was asked recently whether spiritual experiences come from mental illness, and I can understand why some people think the answer is yes. Sometimes these experiences can occur after a trauma such as a nervous breakdown, but a spiritualist may describe this as a spiritual awakening. To those who have not developed themselves spiritually, they explain this away by reasoning that people who practise connecting with the spirit world, praying to God, or believing in angels or guides and masters are delusional. Yet Jesus said, "I am the way, the truth, and the life." When you consider the details of his life as documented in the Bible, Jesus couldn't have given a clearer directive as far as spiritual experiences are concerned. To this day, many people label spiritual or religious experiences as having manifested in the minds of mentally ill people. But it should be commonly accepted that miracles still take place in the lives of people who have not been diagnosed with a mental illness

Three Parts of Spiritual Experiences

Mind: Many spiritualists or mediums see a divine white light when experiencing a connection with the higher dimensions or higher vibrations that exist around us. Some see visions in the third eye. I saw in my third eye a whole herd of unicorns heading towards me. It was a pleasant experience and not at all scary. Some people see manifestations of those who have died and now exist as spirits. Some see coloured orbs. Those standing nearby can witness these things.

Body: Energy centres that resonate with various coloured rays exist within our bodies; angelic beings and ascended masters can use these to connect with us on different levels. Reiki practitioners, for example, can see the coloured rays. Recognizing this and balancing our energy centres will enhance our health and happiness to its optimum state. Our creativity can increase, followed by changes in our lives on a soul level (i.e., our souls can expand, as they advance by learning valuable lessons on their journeys in life).

Spirit: Connecting with the spirit enables us to deal with past mistakes (karma). When we see mistakes as lessons, it gives us the opportunity to forgive the people we have offended and vice versa. All good acts are registered in the spirit world on a soul level, thereby creating good karma. Returning to earth through different lifetimes will, in turn, expand our souls through karmic cleansing until there is no need to return to earth. This is the case if we have learned our soul lessons and our spirits have risen to the highest level possible.

So, if the mind, body, and spirit are balanced, you will likely have spiritual and religious experiences that appear to others who once put you in the delusional category.

Balancing

Spiritualists believe in practising kindness to others. Although this is a basic human gift from the entity or spirit energy we call God, it is not always easy to carry out because we humans have lower as well as higher selves, so it is a balancing act of sorts. Our higher self lifts our thoughts towards goodness and kindness, while our lower self pulls them down towards greed and selfishness. These human emotions are constantly within us. So, a spiritualist would argue that it is necessary to strive for thoughts that lift us towards God and the universal, or *ki*, energy. It is good for our minds, bodies, and souls, and it helps us lead happier lives. We are then endeavouring to reach what God wants for us and what we want to achieve for ourselves.

This push and pull is with us throughout our lives on earth. It is important that we seek out and enjoy the natural gifts of our planet by respecting the trees, flowers, animals, insects, rivers, oceans, and our fellow human beings in our work and home environments. As difficult as this can be, the returns could be enormous. If every person brings about conscious changes, the conscious vibrations of earth will rise, and there will be a return to the golden age that existed on earth thousands of years ago, as in the time of Atlantis. Surely this is not mental illness but pureness of heart being manifested.

When you study cause and effect and soul development, it all makes sense, but understanding these things on a human level does not happen overnight.

The dead poet Frank Dickinson made contact with me over thirty years ago and he told me some beautiful poetry. But I do believe the following words of one particular poem still hold a very important message for us all today. It added meaning to my life, so I will share the statement with you: "Love must be born in the universe, or life becomes meaningless, mindless, or worse."

Do You Believe You Have a Soul?

A friend asked me if I believed I had a soul. She then asked me to answer several questions to help her with a course she was doing. My response follows each question.

Q: "Do you believe you have a soul?"

C: "Yes, I believe I have a soul."

Q: "What do you imagine is the purpose of the soul?"

C: "To know itself experientially."

Q: "What are your thoughts about the place of the soul in the conduct of human affairs?"

C: "I believe the place of the soul is to serve as an ultimate higher self that can draw upon the experience of other lives it has incarnated into.

"I also believe the soul's broader reason contributes to its eternal existence – past, present, and future – of feeling, knowing, loving, sharing, and enjoying its individual and collective experience of itself. It can serve as a base for spiritual growth of any given life or lives it experiences. I believe it is possible for the soul to connect with two lives or more at the same time, because time does not exist on a soul level; it is just a continuum. And each soul contributes to the development of humankind on earth as well as on other planets, stars, and universes."

Q: "What is the relationship of your soul to God, as you understand it?"

C: "It is my link with a kind and incredibly intelligent being that knows my thoughts, words, and deeds and communicates with me on a level that I can understand. This being is enlightening and has a sense of humour."

Q: "If you believe we each have a soul, do you think it is possible for your soul to communicate with mine at a level that transcends physicality? Do you believe that our souls have the ability to communicate in the same way as God?"

C: "Yes, I do believe this, as we are all one. But in our physical, linear lives we are not aware of this."

Past-Life Regression

After I facilitated a past-life regression session for someone and accessed a few of my own previous lives, I began wondering about their authenticity. I turned to G for his truth on this subject; his response is set out below:

C: "Do people truly visit one of our own previous incarnations when a therapist takes us through a regression?"

G: "When you undergo regression, you are taken to a natural state of the subconscious mind. This is where your past lives may be accessed. The authenticity of any given life should be accepted if the client trusts the therapist and his or her work. The therapist should have certain qualifications to confirm the truth in what he or she is hears from the client."

C: "Thank you for explaining. It is becoming clearer. May I ask you, then – is it possible that we are connecting with a collective consciousness belonging to that particular soul's life?"

G: "It is possible, yes. You must remember that it is also possible that a client who has been regressed may adopt the persona and reality of another person."

C: "Isn't this rather dangerous then?"

G: "No, because when you trust the therapist who helped you reach that level of the soul through the regression process, you should feel safe. This type of work requires the client to be of sound mind."

C: "Is there any way to prove the authenticity?"

G: "If a fairly recent life is accessed – say, one from fifty to one hundred years ago – the facts could be proven by seeking them out in libraries, newspapers, visits to homes occupied by the person, church and hospital records, and so on.

        "I do hope this clarifies the topic."

C: "Yes, thank you. Your replies have helped a great deal."

CHAPTER 2

How to Contact Angels

Darren Linton, chapter author

Why Is There an Increased Interest in Angels?

Most of us are aware of the challenges facing the world. The angels are here in record numbers to help humans during these important times and lead us into a bright and better future. Many believe that 2012 heralded the dawn of a new era of humankind and the planet and that the divine source sends energies and angels to assist in the transformation of the world. These are exciting times! Angels can provide us with wise and loving guidance to improve our own lives, help others, and create a better world for everyone.

Do You Wonder Why You Haven't Connected Fully with Your Angels?

Anyone can learn how to connect with his or her angels and hear them. Then you can receive their endless love, wisdom, answers, and guidance to help you improve your life (and the lives of others). You will feel so loved and blessed by the wisdom and love from angels. It is a wonderful experience.

Many people ask their angels for help. No doubt you have received some signs and answers already; otherwise, you probably wouldn't be reading this book. You may have found feathers or parking spaces or had prayers answered in amazing ways. Perhaps you have received answers from angels via a song, a page in a magazine or book, an unexpected phone call from a friend, or in a thousand other possible ways. It is good to know that they are there, helping us.

Like anything else, learning to talk with your angels takes a time and practice, and you can take a course to help you. If you wanted to learn, for example, Reiki, mediumship, reflexology, other forms of healing, or almost anything, you might similarly expect to attend a weekend course or longer and practise what you learn.

How Do the Angels Help Us?

Angels help us in many ways. They can provide healing, visions, direct guidance, and answers. They can intervene to help events turn out well or provide love and protection. They can send healing and positive energies to help us, and they can perform miracles.

Look for Signs

Over the next few days, look for visions and dreams, helpful strangers, recurring numbers and symbols, or any of the other signs mentioned above. These are signs of angels.

Darren Linton, the author of this chapter, runs courses throughout the year and can be contacted via his website at the end of this book.

CHAPTER 3

Guardian Angels, Spirit Guides, Souls, and Dimensions

Angel holding ball of light
Shape shifts to dragon/mermaid

Your Guardian Angel

A guardian angel stays with you for your soul's lifetime, however many incarnations you experience. These are often loved ones who have passed over and then come into your life to guide you, depending upon their evolutionary level and growth. Many of our loved ones do help guide us, but they are not our main guides.

Spirit Guides

Spirit guides are another name for human energy that has lived many lifetimes. These beings have acquired great knowledge and wisdom, and they agree to assist people in whatever way they can. Spirit guides also offer love and wisdom and help you reach your full potential. They can direct your life, and they will always answer your questions. These beings offer inner knowledge and peace, but they will not make choices for you. You are the creator of your life.

You will have one main guide, often referred to as the doorkeeper. This guide is with you for your entire lifetime, and he or she cannot be a member of the family who you ever knew because the person is appointed at your birth.

Other guides will assist you with different phases of your life, depending on your needs at any particular time—for example, practical, emotional, spiritual, and so forth. If you are drawn to different spiritual interests on your journey, such as Egyptian, Shamanism, crystals, or spiritual healing, you will experience the energies of particular guides with knowledge of that tradition.

Soul

Each individual's soul experience and evolution affects the vibration at which each person operates and which vibratory level our guides work at. The more experiences we have, the more we work on becoming the best we can be—who we truly are—the higher our vibration goes. And then the guides who have higher vibrations will be able to work with us.

Dimensions

We live and work in the third dimension, during which time we vibrate at the third dimension. However, when we relax, go into a trance, sleep, or meditate, we vibrate at the fourth dimension, the level where many guides operate and where most peoples' loved ones exist. We can access the higher vibrations, such as the fifth, sixth, seventh, and even eighth dimensions if we are in a deeper trance or if we are more evolved. Within each dimension, there are many levels of vibration. That is why we can sense different types of energies emitted by different guides.

Angel Signs

As I write this book, there is a heatwave in the United Kingdom. It is July and 80 degrees Fahrenheit. The sky is blue, the birds are singing, and the flowers in my garden are blooming. Time for a short break in the countryside, plus it would avoid the inevitable crush on the motorway to the seaside resorts. I hadn't been to Guildford for about twenty years, so booking into the smart new Radisson for the weekend there was a wonderful break. I couldn't help asking when I checked in what the room number would be. I smiled when told it was 343 adding up to 10 which is meaningful for me.

Doreen Virtue has published a pocket-sized book called *Angel Numbers* that gives the divine meaning to any number that can appear when you start asking the angel realm for guidance (this is like a parallel universe where the angels exist on different levels). Many people around the world have stories of clearly seeing, for example, a clock face with the hands stuck on 6.00 p.m., followed by something significant happening that day at 6.00 p.m. This is often your angel communicating with you.

Three is also a very significant number to me, and it repeatedly comes up when the angels want to give me a sign that all is going well. They truly are amazing. These little signs and incidents of repeated numbers contribute to our belief in the angels and their wish to help us and guide us towards the best things in our lives. So, at the hotel, I quietly gave thanks and knew the weekend would be perfect. It was a memorable time of walking round town, visiting Guildford Castle, the river, little coffee shops, and quaint cobbled streets, and the sun shone non-stop.

These are the types of actions that happen when you start working with the angelic realms. And remember to always say thank you to the angels.

The Three Cherry Trees

In 2011, I awoke one morning to see a full-colour vision on my bedroom. The leaves were vibrant green, and they had what looked like red apples scattered all over. I stared in amazement until I grew tired, and the vision disappeared. If I hadn't seen it with my own eyes, I might never have believed it. As time went by, I forgot about my vision, despite wondering what it meant.

The following spring, the same full-colour vision appeared in the same place, but this time I asked what it was and why it appeared to me. A spirit messenger told me that the angels would like me to plant a cherry tree for the birds. "Ah!" I thought, "So they are not red apples. They are cherries." I made enquiries about the cost of a tree and planned where I would plant it. I drew a coloured picture of the cherry tree in my diary and wrote a note beside it to buy one. But before long, the planting season passed, so I vowed to plant one the following autumn.

I soon forgot about the cherry tree, but the angelic realm did not. On 1 September 2013, the same brightly coloured vision appeared in the same place on my ceiling, and I felt a pang of guilt. How could I have failed to plant the tree that the angels wanted for the birds? At this point, my spirit guide told me that a wonderful being had brought me the vision.

I looked on the Internet and asked about trees at a couple of garden centres, but the ones that were left looked tatty. As a last resort, I went to a bigger garden centre suggested by my daughter, and I was pleased to find a magnificent row of Morello cherry trees. Without wasting any time, I bought the tree and compost and planted the cherry tree that weekend. I prayed that it would blossom and produce many luscious and healthy cherries for the birds to eat!

The Number Five

When I book a hotel room and I am allocated room number five or it will be divisible by five, such as ten, fifteen, or twenty. This is a definite sign that our angels are constantly working behind the scenes. For example, a forthcoming visit to Malta has been booked for a stay on the fifth floor! I often say a silent thank you to the angels, as I am bolstered by their efforts at influencing this serendipity to take place and letting us know that blessings will generally follow.

I have lost count of the times that the angels have arranged for my partner, Paul, and me to stay in a room related to the number five, so I will not belabour this point. Recently, this message has extended to family members as well.

My mother-in-law fell ill on a visit to her family in Scotland over Christmas 2011. She was already being treated for a lung infection, so we expected the travelling would be hard on her. Little did we know that she would spend the whole of Christmas in hospital, where she remained into January 2012. At one point, it was touch-and-go whether she would make it through to the New Year. We prayed hard to the angels and God to give her the strength to get well and come back to us healthy again. Through the power of prayer, she returned to London at the end of January. On our first visit to see her in the local hospital, we were amazed to find that she was in bed number five. In the bed next to her was a lady whose first name was Angel, a very spiritual woman. It was more proof from the Angels.

On the other side of Joan, my mother-in-law, there was a kind lady who was pregnant, and we all prayed for her to be healed of asthma. She used breathing equipment daily, so she needed help from God and the angels to get through this difficult time. Unfortunately, we could not follow her outcome, as she was moved to a maternity ward, but there is no doubt in my mind that she received help from heaven and earth.

Angelic Bank Holiday

One bank holiday was also Paul's birthday, so we spent the weekend in Bath, a place of great historical interest. It is situated in a valley, and our hotel was on the edge of town. The angels arranged for us to stay in a room that added up to ten! We couldn't help but smile when the manager handed us keys to room number nineteen. We had a great weekend. The weather was sunny, and we sampled the new spa there, supplied daily with forty-two minerals from underground spring water pumped up to the roof level.

The following week, I was walking along a quiet road with a friend of mine. There were only a few clouds in the sky, but as I looked skyward, I saw a cloud clearly shaped like the number 301. I asked my friend what she saw, and she described the numeral 301. When I returned home, I looked these numbers up in Doreen Virtue's *Angel Numbers* and was delighted to see that seeing 301 means that God and the ascended masters ask you to keep your thoughts of love focussed on the positive. The central numeral, zero, means that God is talking to you. I said a silent thank you for this further confirmation that God and the angels were communicating with me. Anyone can do this. Just keep your eyes and ears open for any numbers that repeat themselves; it could be the angels communicating with you.

One Saturday started with a visit to a fairy festival with my daughter in West Sussex, and the rain fortunately held off. Because I suffer from arthritis in my spine, rainy periods tend to be quite painful for me, as my muscles and bones react. Moving on, I give special thanks to my daughter for discovering angel eye cream at one stall there, as it worked a treat on the dark circles under my eyes!

The following day I did some DIY painting, and the next day I was in pain. After waking up and aching badly all over my back, shoulders, neck, and head, I decided in desperation to try the EFT tapping method, whereby you tap on acupressure points. I learned a version of this at qigong where I was taught by a qualified trainer to place the palm of my hand on my forehead tapping with my fingers then repeating the same action on the brow, under the collar bone and under the arm. You can continue to your shoulders, legs, feet, and lower back. When I used this method, I felt much better within minutes. It is also good for mild headaches, neck aches, and neuralgia (only gentle tapping should be done on the face).

This technique is being heralded as the latest method of self-healing in the United States and United Kingdom. As it's self-administered, it doesn't cost a penny – only your time. Any seriously arthritic people should check with their doctor before using a new method like this. However, I have tried it, and it has caused me no harm.

An Angel Encounter

I was having a cappuccino in a local DIY store at the time of the Queen's Diamond Jubilee, when I noticed that the man opposite was reading something on his mobile phone and holding his head in his other hand. He looked worried, so I asked my guardian angel what was wrong with the man. She said that his mother was in another country and very sick, but he could not be with her. She told me to look more closely at the area around his head. As I did, I saw the aura around his head stand out, and it was glowing white. The man moved his head back quickly, and the light behind it stayed in the shape of his head and shone like a bright light. My angel told me that this was his guardian angel consoling him. The light I could see was his angel's manifestation. She added that he did not have the money to visit his mother and that was why he was so down. I watched the man relax and lean back to finish the rest of his mobile message.

Although I will never know the outcome of his mother's sickness or whether he managed to visit her, I feel comforted to have witnessed this happen. It reinforced my belief that angels can and do help us with and without our knowledge.

Goddess Brigid

Goddess in the Sky

As I walked along one morning, past the shopping centre near where I live, it was raining and there were dark clouds in the sky. Suddenly, it stopped raining. As I glanced upwards, the dark clouds parted, and the sun shone from between them. I quickly took a photo, and looking through the lens, I saw a figure jump into view. I was later told by my guide that it was Goddess Brigid, known to have evolved from various deities in the past to a modern-day goddess of peace and unity. She is a Catholic saint who works for the good of all. As I have been a lightworker for some years now, I was very grateful to her for appearing to me. It served as an incredible validation the following weekend, as I was booked into an earth angels holistic fair in Belfast, Northern Ireland, and many there believed in Goddess Brigid. She is an inspiration for the people of Ireland and the world.

AFFIRMATION

Each morning for a short while, I imagine being lifted up into a realm of angels who help keep a feeling of harmony with me through my day.

CHAPTER 4

God Works in Mysterious Ways

The same soul can exist in various personalities and different time periods. The stories in this chapter show some uncanny ways that the loving, caring universe we live in can respond when a pet passes on or when something goes missing.

A Tale of Two Cats

A friend told me this story, and it proves how our pets are in spirit to us as well as the indelible mark they leave on our hearts and souls. I have heard numerous tales of cats, dogs, and horses that have passed away later reappearing to their owners to reassure them and to let them know that they are now in a happy place.

Jan's Cat

Jan said, "A strange thing about Tom a couple of days before he died, he took to lying behind the door in the living room. He hadn't really been out properly for weeks. That night, his double appeared outside our kitchen windowsill. He always had a habit of sitting there when he wanted to come in. It really spooked me, because I knew it couldn't be him, and there had never been any other tabbies in the area.

"And then, on the day he died, I saw his double fly across the garden. It made a mad dash with the wind under his tail, just like my cat used to do when he was younger. He was quite a distinctive tabby, with white socks and bib, and this cat was his double. As I was standing, watching, another very similar cat followed it across the lawn. I thought I was going mad at this point.

"After my cat died, I didn't see the cats again, so I felt the ones I saw must have been cat spirits. Then, one day, looked at my cat's grave where we'd put a cat statue, and suddenly the first tabby appeared and rubbed itself around the statue.

"Anyway, it turns out that two tabby brothers moved into the area, and they are both very affectionate and spend quite a bit of time in the garden. They are like the answer to a prayer and such a comfort. It is so strange that they looked so much like my cat. I believe I have been touched by angels."

This could have been a case of mistaken identity, but it's strange that one of the new tabbies took on the role of Jan's old one. Had he been sent to comfort my friend?

Zoe's Cat

My daughter told me this second tale of possible feline mistaken identity. She was living in the Canary Islands at the time, where many cats roam wild and free; in some cases this is because they were abandoned by their owners when leaving the island for good. This story involved Zoe's much-loved pet, Tom.

Zoe is a great animal lover. While she was living in Spain, she had a dog and three stray cats; she ensured that they were all well fed and allowed them to come and go as they pleased. Tom, the very first one she adopted, had distinct colourings of ginger and white. About a year previous to when she told me this story, he had disappeared for quite a number of days. This is not unusual for a cat, but some while later, she was pulling up outside the villa where she lived, and there was Tom lying motionless in the road. She got out of her car, picked him up, and carried him indoors, feeling very upset, as he was very special to her. He kept Zoe company when her husband worked late.

Later that day, they did what they thought was the best thing and buried Tom in their garden, said a little prayer, and went off to bed. She told me that she had cried inconsolably that night. Tom had been her first pet after arriving in the Canary Islands, and he had lived with them for six years. The very next day, however, Tom appeared through the back door. At first she was shocked and then amazed and pleased, to say the least. The only conclusion we could come to was that the dead cat that had never been seen in the area before must have been Tom's brother. We agreed that it was no coincidence that he was killed outside his brother's home.

The final cat story is particularly touching, as my friend was so upset because she couldn't be with her pet to say goodbye, but what a twist in the tale!

She said, "My cat died, and an identical cat came into my house the next day and died in my cat's bed. My cat had died at the vet's, and I hadn't been able to gather the strength to see him one last time, so I left the arrangements to my nephew."

I have included these stories about people and their pets because animals have souls too, and we will meet the animals we have loved when we pass on into the spirit world. Our guardian angels and guides often have a hand in easing the pain of our pets passing to let us know that they are still being cared for on the other side. Pets give us love and companionship, and in return, their only needs are food, warmth, kindness, and love. This is something to bear in mind as we humans may overspend, overeat, and overwork to satisfy our greedy desires. Taking care of plants, trees, wildlife, animals, and others will satisfy our hearts, minds, and souls long after we pass on.

Group Souls

Our soul energy is part of a combined soul group which works together for the evolution of the group. Somehow, we may meet up with members of our soul group when we incarnate into any given lifetime. These meetings are predestined and designed by our soul, our guides, angels, and the universe to move us forward on our spiritual path and can include animals as well as humans.

The following story shows that when we open ourselves to connect with the angels around us, they help us in turn to meet up with members of our soul group or like minded people spreading more light around our world.

Cate

Although Cate was a complete stranger to me we both felt a meeting of spiritual minds.

I was driving to an appointment at our local hospital and was unsure of how to get there. I pulled over to ask for help when Cate poked her head through the window. She told me she worked in the Unit I was on my way to, so I offered her a lift. "What a coincidence," I thought and we both laughed. At the check-in desk, I was told no appointment had been made for 9.00 a.m. that day. "How strange," I thought. But Cate had a word with the booking clerk and they fitted me in. I sat down to read the book I had brought with me which was *What God Wants* and

Cate asked me what it was about I gave a brief description and then she told me about a spiritual experience she had as a child.

When Cate was six years old, her family had moved into an old house in Scotland. On this particular day she was alone and remembered seeing a male ghost at the end of the long corridor. It was dressed in black robes, wore a funny old hat, and carried a wooden staff that had the head of an eagle on top. A catholic priest was called into the house who said that Cate had seen Burick, a member of the local landed gentry who lived in the house hundreds of years before. Cate had been more intrigued than frightened by the ghost and I agreed that ghosts intrigue me but I accept they are merely shadows from the past that do not exist on earth as we do.

Barbara

On another occasion, I met Barbara, a very kind and gentle-spirited lady. We had both been to an Alternatively Speaking evening in Shirley, Surrey. We got along very well, and I taught and attuned her to the first two levels of Reiki, which opened up a whole new world for her. The following story about Barbara's son once again proves that we are being looked after by our spirit guides.

Michael's Key

Barbara's son, Michael, had lost the key to a house he let out, and it was important that he find it to get in and do some urgent repairs. When I received a voicemail from Barbara, I went into action. I spoke with my guides and received a message that the missing key was in Michael's jacket. I phoned Barbara and told her, but when they looked in all his jackets, they couldn't find the key. This left us all disappointed. Later that day, I asked my spirit guides again where his key was and why it had not been found, but I received the same message again, "It's in his jacket." A few days later, Barbara left another phone message for me, saying the key had been found in a leather jacket covered by another coat on their kitchen chair.

Sha-Ra

Another time, Barbara asked me to draw her spirit guide. I put my request out and waited for the guide to appear. A few weeks later, the head and shoulders of a man with an Aztec appearance told me his name was Sha-ra, and he was Barbara's guide. I drew him, and he gave me a wonderful message for Barbara, but that's not the end of the story.

Barbara asked me to help Michael again when he applied for a particular job. I said it would be better if Michael and Barbara asked their guides and angels themselves, but I asked my guides to help Michael too. Sadly, he didn't get that job. The spirit world had another job for Michael, so we were amazed when he was successful with the next job he applied for, and the name of the company was Scarab! We all thought it strange that scarab beetles would have been around at the time of Sha-ra, who must have had a hand in finding Michael's job!

AFFIRMATION

Being kind and compassionate to children, animals, and nature raises my spiritual consciousness and opens my awareness of angel energy in every form of life.

CHAPTER 5

Angels, Dimensions, Chakras, and Auras

Angel Flying Upwards

I wrote the following poems to help people focus on their inner light and to meditate with the purpose and intention of bringing specific qualities of the archangels into their lives. It is essential that you ground your energies by drawing your energy down from above and around you. Ask for protection from the archangel Michael and your guardian angel. Then imagine a golden or white light coming down through your crown chakra (the top of your head). Gently breathe in through your nose and out through your mouth; this will raise your vibrational energy level. Followers of qigong tend to favour breathing in and out through your mouth, which sends more oxygen into your brain, but take it easy at first.

In your mind, picture anchoring your energy to three large rocks at the centre of the earth. If you cannot visualise this, just think about the idea. Say the words, "I am drawing up mother earth energy," and imagine it happening if you like. Breathe in gently and visualise the energy coming up through the soles of your feet and into your earth-star and soul-star chakras (below and above your body) to balance your energies. It takes some practice, but any little step towards meditating and grounding your energies is a move towards bringing more light into the world for the highest good of all.

To open yourself to the angelic realms, sit and quietly play some very gentle music and light a small candle to focus your mind. At first, you can recite and meditate on the rainbow poem and ask your angels to draw near. It will help balance the energy centres in your body.

Angel Rainbow Meditation

Breathe in deeply; meditate
Into contemplative state.
Let your thinking freely roam.
Ask the angels to be shown

As angels' chakras' coloured hues,
Yellow, green, red, and blue,
Infuse and fill your atmosphere,
Making life become more clear.

Archangels resonate with particular colours of our chakras (energy centres). If you feel drawn to a certain colour, read my archangel poems. Ask for the help of a specific archangel for guidance in your life for the particular quality you need at the time.

The chakra colours of archangels have changed because practising spiritualists now live and work in the fifth dimension of vibrational energy.

The Different Dimensions

The Third Dimension
This is the densest part of this plane, containing our own worldly and material thoughts.

The Fourth Dimension
This dimension is the place of truth, also called the astral plane.

It is a grey, polarized plane, housing the forces of light and darkness. It's where we go in when we are asleep and where entities exist.

The Fifth Dimension
Called heaven, or the plane of light. The fifth dimension is the highest realm a soul can reach.

The twelve chakras (energy centres of our body), when fully opened, can empower anyone to their energy levels. It is not essential to know their colour rays, but focussing on them helps with meditation.

I dedicate the next poem to 2014 and onwards, to the golden age to come. When I read this poem back to myself after finishing it and closed my eyes, I saw a golden ball of light appear. As it went round in my third-eye vision in a circle, I felt a calm energy fill my body. The ball of light completed its circle, and then light spread across my entire third eye. This golden light is now available for us to draw into our aura, creating an auric egg. Some may see the golden light that descends from that sphere we call heaven.

Golden Light

I start my day the same old way
With praise for thee, because you see

The things in life that are so wrong.
Then, suddenly, I hear a song.

Your angels bring a message clear,
And soon enough, clouds disappear.

I end my day another way.
You send your golden light to play

Upon my soul and through my heart.
Another day dawns to start.

The golden ray resonates with the Christ within us and surrounds us with the energy of Master Jesus.

Archangel Zadkiel
Violet Crown Chakra

Starlight sprinkles into view
Violet-coloured-chakra hue.
Looking upwards through your mind;
Downwards thoughts, the loving kind.

Silent dreams from heaven's veil
Drift to you on the angel's sail.
A taste of peace pervades all truth
With gentle music, soft and smooth.

Archangel Zadkiel inspires harmony, wisdom, divine grace, angelic rapture and spiritual knowledge.

The violet flame is associated with St Germain, the master alchemist. His spiritual teachings expound on the use of the violet flame to transmute negativity to protect us and help us overcome addictive behaviours.

Archangel Raziel
Third-Eye Chakra

As you breathe in the six-point star,
Your visual angel from afar
Shines with wings of brilliant white
Like stars that twinkle through the night,

Mystic magic emanates,
Opening heaven's universal gates.
Your mind enraptured, struck with awe,
As third-eye chakra opens its door.

Archangel Raziel helps raise psychic perception and manifestation, and he can inspire intuition and mystical meaning.

Archangel Raphael now has charge of the third eye at the fifth dimension, for those working at this level who helps with healing of our third eye.

For clarification purposes Archangel Raphael and Archangel Raziel are two separate Archangels.

Archangel Michael
Throat Chakra

At blue throat chakra, Michael waits
Hears your wishes, contemplates
Swiftly answering your call
Protecting you from any fall

Ask his help, see his hue
Eyes of steel so blue and true
Action comes protecting schemes
Bringing life to plans and dreams

Archangel Michael brings strength and protection. He helps remove fear and raises courage and can bring practical help to technical problems.

Archangel Raphael
Green Chakra

As angels weave their heavenly loom,
Their sweetened perfume fills the room.
A healing moment locked in time
When pink and green begin to twine.

Then, as your heart is opened true,
Your chakra centre is known to you.
With others, share your loving found
As deepened feelings release unbound

Archangel Raphael brings love, peace, and harmony. He inspires healers and helps remove additions and cravings.

The pink ray of Archangel Chamuel now has charge of the heart chakra at the fifth dimension.

Archangel Jophiel
Yellow Solar Plexus Chakra

Sending thoughts to the universe
For Angel Jophiel to reverse.
He slows your pace to recognize,
Brings healthy beauty to your eyes.

Seek his golden-yellow glow.
Ideas and knowledge then will flow.
Illuminate your heart and find
He'll banish fear and clear your mind.

Archangel Jophiel inspires happiness, creates powerful energy, and can slow you down to appreciate beauty.

Archangel Gabriel
Sacral Chakra

Send thoughts into the atmosphere,
Where all creation becomes clear.
Transformed to feelings all around,
Angelic wings express the sound.

Create and form your message true,
Helped by Gabriel to you.
Angelic-orange chakra glow
Delivering truth to all below.

Archangel Gabriel is related to expression of talents and overcoming fear; he also encourages action for creative projects and sexual drive.

Archangel Uriel
Solar Plexus Chakra

Send out thoughts to the universe,
But gently breathe. This must come first.
Archangel Uriel's flame will glow
As he supports your way to go.

Then through these insights, signs, ideas,
Problems solved, dispelling fears,
His glowing resonance of red.
Your spirit gently will be fed.

Archangel Uriel supports our creative area, showing the way forward through insights, writing, ideas, and problem solving.

AFFIRMATION

**I connect with the angels and become a
channel of God's universal love.**

CHAPTER 6

Your Planet Earth

I joined Darren Linton's broadcast on Soul Radio for his first Downpouring of Light meditation on 7 April 2011 which involved breathing gently in and out and then listeners were asked to imagine we were drawing down loving pink light. Next we were asked to surround planet earth with divine white light. During the fifteen minutes of meditation I felt a strong connection as I linked with the angels. Can you imagine the strength of this outpouring of divine energy, with angels connecting to some 11,000 lightworkers around the world? At the time of this writing, my thoughts went to Nelson Mandela. He dedicated his life to world peace and recently passed on to spirit, where he is now without doubt truly at peace.

The following poem flowed into my mind. You may want to use it in your own meditations to help raise the light of planet earth, which in turn will bring about world peace in futures yet unknown.

With your help, we can make it happen.

Planet Earth Needs Light

Raise the light of earth
To bring about rebirth.
Masters of all faiths,
Humankind of every race,
With help from beings of light,
Your minds will join the flight.
Like brave hearts now renewed,
Your souls will be imbued.
Rise up those of gentle nature.
Rise up and know your creator.
All life will then excel.
Enlightened hearts will tell
The prophecy divine.
Your hearts and minds will shine.

Golden Light and the Golden Age

We can bring about benefits for ourselves, friends, family, colleagues, and those in control of our financial situations – banks, employers, or savings institutions. Requesting and sending golden light to these areas of our lives can and will make a positive difference, but are we ready to make this commitment? It doesn't take up a great deal of time. A thought, meditation, or kind deed here and there makes a difference, and our joint efforts can reach the targets and bring about the changes needed. In the coming months and years, changes in governmental policies and environmental issues will affect us. With our present systems already breaking down, people are turning towards more spiritual ways of life.

The end of the Mayan calendar in 2012 brought a turning point to a new way of life; it triggered an increase in the outpouring of golden light being brought closer to us via angels, guides, masters, and our creator. This help is as arriving because the need to respect our landscape, animals, and a loving way of life has been lost. More people are dissatisfied with their lives today, despite many having lovely homes, iPhones, iPads, flat-screen TVs, computers, laptops, up-to-the minute gadgetry, and smart lifestyles. It's a slow process, but step-by-step, a better way of living will come.

Keep It Simple

I always try to keep in mind the advice, "keep it simple," whatever I am doing and particularly in relation to meditating. Many people shy away from meditation and want to run a mile if they hear the word. They simply do not understand the true meaning. Meditating means to concentrate fully on any one subject, using most of one's mind. Playing gentle music with a simple melody while you quieten your innermost thoughts this will create the right atmosphere for angels and guides to come close to you. Placing a simple rose quartz crystal nearby can also help, spritz the area with some aura room and space clearing spray (clears the Aura, Room and Surroundings from Negative energy which lingers in our Auras' and environments) then let your thoughts drift away, you are now meditating; just sitting and not thinking of anything is a good way to start!

Asking for the Gold Ray of Christ

The next time you sit down for a quiet time, you can ask for the gold ray of Christ to surround you. Just think, "I am the gold ray of Christ, flowing through my body with wisdom, love, and healing surrounding me with golden light three times." Then ask for this light to go to anyone or any location that you believe is in need of light. If even a million people did this around the world, it would make a difference. End by saying thank you to God and the universe.

Light and Dark

Because lightworkers have focused healing light, love, and joy into many dark places around the world, negative energy around the world has shifted. Men, women, and children need to learn how to bring light into their spaces and local areas so that worldwide purification continues to take place.

The cosmic changes have created floods that will continue until the purification is complete. Tsunamis and earthquakes have caused people to show support and kindness to their fellow humans, helping them find their ability to overcome the worst kinds of tragedies. There has also been worldwide suffering beyond all previous realities. White Eagle my spirit guide tells me that there is a plan behind all the devastation. Therefore, sending light to areas when we hear about tragedies there helps bring about purification on a massive scale.

The Major Shift – 21 December 2012

On a visit to Mexico I met descendants of the Mayan empire, I got to thinking more about the end of the Mayan calendar. The dancer pictured at the beginning of this chapter represents the Mayan sun, still greatly revered by Mexicans to this day. When I returned to the United Kingdom, I was asked what was to happen after 21 December 2012 (the date that marked the end of the Mayan calendar) and how it would affect us.

An intensive cleansing taking place around the world has been eliminating the impurities in nature that cloud human souls and physical bodies. Our attitudes and priorities will change, step by step, for the good. The sun, rain, wind, and snow are each a cleansing phenomenon. "Thank God," I hear you say. That's what we will all be doing twenty years from now, thanking God. But before this more spiritually enhanced world arrives, long-term pollution will cause suffering through the return of some of the old diseases such as bronchitis, mumps, and tuberculosis.

The Good News

The twenty-first century will be marked down in history as a golden and holy period. As we develop a more spiritual way of life, we will find new ways to overcome disease, (dis-ease) but after the massive cleansing, we will begin to show more respect and appreciation for nature in a humble way. This will lead to individuals, families, communities, and the hierarchy acknowledging that everyone is made up of a mind, body, spirit, and soul. Then we will live healthier lives and in the way that God truly intended us to: as humble and loving people, caring and teaching our children to act this way towards each other and all fellow human beings.

I asked G for his comments on the following subject of how we can eat more healthily by not eating meat or food produced by using genetically

modified organisms. I was told that scientists are now producing safe
food products that have been divinely inspired from the spirit world

Concerns About Genetically Modified Foods

Many fast foods we eat are genetically altered during the manufacturing
process. A specific gene is now in use for this purpose in many countries.
The manufacturers claim they can now produce, for example, a sweeter-
tasting tomato in a variety of colours that will grow bigger, last longer,
and be healthier for the consumer.

I asked G for his view on this subject, he replied, "GMO food has been
inspired from the spirit realm because of animal-contaminated food. It
is the way forward for planet earth. It is not only uneconomical to eat
the flesh of animals but also potentially damaging to humans in the
long run."

"Time will show that accepting this form of supplying energy to
humans is a much cleaner and healthier way to go forward into the
next millennium."

I then asked, "People around the world are concerned that GMOs will
create allergic reactions in some people, toxins that produce disease, and
the loss of some species of wildlife."

I received the reply, "Many innovative ideas that came to man from
the spirit realm have gone through a period of trial and error, which is
to be expected. In the long term, a standard will be established for the
use of GMOs.

"Environmentalists make such an outcry as to ensure the establishments
provide such laws and standards. The natural laws of the universe will
be closely guarded by the spirit world, so that discoveries are only used
to the advantage of all humankind."

As our products, animals, and plant life are injected with live genes to prevent disease, we can pray to the spirits that any errors are minimised. All lightworkers around the world can be active in this, requesting that those scientists who hold the key to genetics are guided by the spiritual world to an ultra-perfected form of creation manifested on earth.

The Source and Galactic Guidance

Various theories are being put forward by channellers, trance mediators, mystics, mediums, psychics, healers, and scientists claiming that the source of all light and energy as we know it originated billions or trillions of years ago, and our universe was among others created by the source. The latest theory is that the source created twelve gods and sent them out to different planets to create life there so that the source could know itself within and without experientially. One of these gods was our God, known to us through Christ Jesus – also known as the Christos energy that works through us individually (if we choose to invite this energy into our lives). This is a short version of how and why we are here, but many believe that we are not meant to know and do not need to know more than this until we pass on from this life. We hope to then rise up to the heavenly realms to join our families and friends who have passed on before us.

During the eventful and memorable years of 2012 and 2013, we returned to the ancient masters and present-day spiritual masters for the best and most beneficial ways to live on earth and fulfil our purpose in this lifetime. This year, lightworkers and potential lightworkers – those who draw down divine white light and energy and pass it on to others through healing –are being afforded the opportunity to commune with energies above and below us. This phenomenon is facilitated by angels, masters, and guides flooding energy to earth to bring necessary changes to humans in need of living better lives as intended when the Source created our God.

So, why not tap into some of this energy during meditation? It's easy once you get started, as I described previously: light a candle and play gentle music to create a nice area where you can sit quietly and just be. Then let your mind wander to the top of your head. Gently breathe in and out, and ask your guardian angel to guide your thoughts forwards and upwards. As you breathe divine white light and energy down into your being, you may say a prayer for someone whom you know needs to be uplifted or even for yourself, and then say thank you to your guardian angel. You can expand on this, but more than this short meditation can be overwhelming for those who have not meditated before. But practised daily, it can work wonders in your life, bringing about fulfilment and focusing your daily aims, if only in little ways at first.

Here are is a list of masters you can ask for help and guidance:

Lakshmi – To help with the flow of prosperity

Buddha – To help with meditation

Isis – To balance career and home life

Apollo – To focus on your strengths

Quan Yin – To help you let go

Mother Mary – To nurture yourself

Jesus – To open your heart to love

There are many more helpers in spirit, but your guardian angel can be your first port of call. Always ask for the protection of Archangel Michael, who is the angel closest to God in relationship and resemblance.

There has never been a better time to get started, so I wish anyone reading these words to give it a try. My guide White Eagle tells me to "keep on keeping on," and you can do the same!

Galactic Channelling

I have chosen to channel messages and information from Ascended Masters, but they also choose to work with me. My guide Kim, who was a Chinese doctor when he incarnated on earth, told me, "I chose you from among many for your sense of right and wrong, your steadfastness, your loyalty, your love of humanity, your desire to help others, and the love in your heart. Also, we have known each other through many lifetimes – through struggles, poverty, and riches; the same thread runs through your heart in this life."

I asked Kim if I would progress much further on my path, as I feel I have learned so much he replied that I would expand my learning and develop a deeper artistic and creative spirit as my soul contact expands. He added that I have the freedom to decide which way to go. He also told me that the reason many mediums follow the route of Jesus Christ, his followers, and ancient masters who join us in our crusade towards the golden age do so because it is a safer route for them.

Many mediums and channellers worldwide are now receiving messages from other galaxies, also communications with Angels, Archangels and Spiritual Beings are becoming widespread. I personally feel a strong connection with Sirius, which is where I believe I have descended from originally. I received a message from a Sirian telling me that our world is caught in an in-between state of reality as heaven prepares to give the green light. A liaison is monitoring what is going to happen soon, and an announcement by our new governance will mark the end of a long era of the controlling darkness, economic upheaval, and widespread discord as it replaces the old regimes. This will probably not occur within the foreseeable future.

Is It Safe to Connect with Other Realities?

The latest spiritual experience available today says that it's safe to connect with other realities, but it can be dangerous to dip into that which we have experienced in another life. Everything takes place at the same time in the spirit world, and there is no timeline, so it must be safe I have been told by my guides.

However, surely we should be in a balanced position mentally before embarking on experiencing these other lifetimes to incorporating their qualities into this one. Courses offer experiences, for example, that a novice singer could enhance skills from a lifetime when he or she was a renowned vocalist. The theory goes that you would have already experienced being an excellent singer in another life, so you can tap into that lifetime to help in this one, and apparently you will be in a safe place. This can be practised in many other applications.

What Is the Difference between Soul and Spirit?

As quantum visits are taking place, most people still have difficulty in discerning the difference between the soul and the spirit. The Bible explains that the spirit is the element in humanity which gives us the ability to have an intimate relationship with God. Therefore, whenever the word "spirit" is used, it refers to the immaterial part of humanity that connects with God, who himself is spirit (see John 4: 24).

The soul, in turn, is a combination of a person's mind, will, intellect, and emotions. Its function is not to reveal but to actively work and choose. Whenever the word "soul" is used, it can refer to the whole person, whether alive or in the afterlife. The soul is the essence of human beings – it is who we are. In its most basic sense, the word "soul" means life.

Quantum experiences are not something that anyone should embark upon lightly. However, in these times of rapidly changing vibrations on our planet, things are changing, and we are assured that further miracles on the soul and spirit levels will be taking place.

AFFIRMATION

**I trust and am told by spirit that all injustice
will be righted in the end.**

CHAPTER 7

White Eagle's Message

W hite Eagle, one of my guides, channelled the following message to me on 1 January 2013:

I have come to deliver this New Year's message of hope – yes hope – for all on planet earth. I bring inspiration to all through your lightworkers who have toiled through 2012. I bring joy, peace, love, and hope to you.

Planetary Changes

Changes will occur on a planetary level undetected by most, but those amongst you with higher knowledge are aware of such occurrences. Jupiter is bringing alignments into a quicker realm of activity. Not being technical now – how does this affect the individuals? It is twofold. Firstly, there will be globally higher sea levels and movements of the mass of earth, shifting tectonic plates and causing devastation. This will be followed by the cleansing etheric and the physical, as the low-lying lands create necessary upheavals of homes and lives affected in this generation. Though not obvious, this is ultimately for the good of all.

On a Basic Level

After the storm comes the calm, a recollection of what was and where to go. For some, moving forward will be hard but necessary. Shattered will pick up the pieces and bear love in their hearts once more.

At Governing Levels

Those in charge of running countries have an awakening to come. This is a must, as not enough has been achieved since the 1980s or 1990s in regard to economics and restructuring of balancing powers for the profit of the poorest amongst you and to benefit the workers.

The Doom and Gloom of No Hope Is Past

Hidden doors are opening now. There will be opportunities for healthier, greener industries to grow and prosper; even the lowest earner will receive gains. Mistakes made in the past will be overcome. By 2014, huge strides will take place on a global scale for health and love in the hearts of mankind to return.

Help from Spirits Is Promised for the Golden Age

We, in spirit, are guiding the achievers amongst you, from the so-called top to bottom of society. Love will conquer all and bring justice back into the world. It will not happen overnight, but it will come to pass. Have faith that goodness and fairness will replace money and materialism where it has been wrongly held in high esteem. Judge not your brother or sister, as you all play your own part in bringing about the golden age. Support each other in the true meaning of the word.

Keep on keeping on, and we in spirit will not fail you.

What a magnificent and inspiring message to receive on the first day of 2013. I feel honoured that I can deliver White Eagle's message to you, the readers.

Moving On

Since the time I received this message from White Eagle, I have seen huge strides being made by the government and financial institutions to bring to task our banks, gas, electricity, insurance companies, and lending bodies as well as local councils and the financial services. These regulations are forcing them to be more honourable in their dealings with us, the paying public. The daily news reports that the watch bodies and ombudsmen are fining and making cash returns to consumers. I have been told that God will straighten all roads, and although we have a long way to go, these words appear to be coming true.

AFFIRMATION

I see the wonder and beauty in nature and know it can be found in the silence of my inner being.

CHAPTER 8

Angels and Elementals

On a sunny day in July 2011, as I walked towards the park, I saw a mass of angelic-shaped clouds. I took a few photos, as it looked like the angels and elementals were painting an unexplainable and complex picture above me. When the photo was developed and saved to my computer, I saw incredible swirling, active humanoid figures in them. The angels told me, "They are saving your soul." People tell me they see different figures in my photos, as the elementals are shifting shapes all the time.

I photographed the Archangel Michael on another day, holding his arm above the head of a spirit. He wore two bracelets, one on the wrist and one below the elbow, with a white ribbon flowing from the wrist down its full-length gown. Behind Michael's shoulder was a ferocious being holding a dagger to the archangel's head. Behind this dark figure a figure that looks similar to Mr T!

The riots that started in Central London on 4 August 2011 and then spread to Croydon and other parts of England. As angry youths smashed their way into shops and banks, burning cars and violently intimidating anyone in their path and helping themselves to luxury goods and cash, the public asked why this was happening.

I believe that like a boil that festers but does not heal until the poison is removed, lower energies have entered the minds of our youth and fuelled their anger. These young people will, of course, regret their actions in time. I hope this happens within our lifetime. Without the goodness of God and the mighty work of his angels and masters filtering into the spirit-minded people of Earth, we would all be mindless creatures who selflessly grab whatever we can from our friends, our neighbours, and our loved ones. It doesn't bear thinking about. So, we turn to God and pray as lightworkers draw down divine light and draw up Mother Earth's energy to bring about peace in the world for all mankind, as the Golden Age must and will come. The proof is in the sky and in the hearts of God-loving people on earth that heaven is working with us.

My Experience with Dragons

I attended a workshop with my grandchildren at a Mind Body Spirit Exhibition in London and they found it a bit of fun as they didn't realize that they were also learning about the elemental world. I had been corresponding with Alphedia of Elemental Beings in Scotland discussing the elementals workshops that she runs. I told her of a recent experience I had with dragons to gain her insight into the vast knowledge that she has on this subject.

> I called on my dragon today, as I heard a flapping noise to the right of my divine altar. I never knew it was my dragon until I went on to your information page.

> I had seen, as I awoke from a dream yesterday, a rock and a green light flowing across it. I think now that it was my dragon.

> My dragon said his name was Justicia (but that sounds feminine; can there be female dragons?). He said he has been with me over the last sixteen years, helping me along my path. In my third eye, I saw my dragon as I was soaking in my hot bath with lavender in it. I can't remember any more than this, as we were interrupted by another spirit.

> There has been a bit of a mystery surrounding this flapping noise, which is sometimes very strong, and knowing that a battle has been going on around where I live in Croydon, I am not surprised that the dragons have been working their socks off.

Ley Lines

The Victorian house I live in is confirmed as being directly in the middle of a very wide ley line (Note: a ley line is a supposed straight line connecting three or more prehistoric or ancient sites, sometimes regarded as the line of a former track and associated with lines of energy and other paranormal phenomena).

This type of proof i.e. where a ley line supposedly existed, was considered important in ancient times when dragons were said to roam the English countryside. An expert used a wooden pendulum to detect the ley line on the green close to where I live and pointed out the direction of the trees as further proof. Their branches take immediate right angles left, right, and downwards, showing how the energy of marching pilgrims affected the tree growth.

There are different types of dragons: red-fire dragons, who I am told should only be called on for their help if you are strong-minded; blue dragons; and green dragons. Once your third eye is opened and you have made contact with yours through meditation, show it the respect and kindness it deserves, and you will be surprised at the help it brings.

As you can see, the elementals are canny creatures that work in liaison with angels, and they help us understand the magical kingdom open to those who let them know we are aware of their existence.

My Dream Dragon

In a dream, I was in a house when I saw a young, soft, cuddly live dragon. He was the size of a small pony and appeared to be living with us. I stroked him, and so did other members of my family throughout this dream. I remember feeling happy that he was there and protected. His skin was light, and his wings were green and closed against his body. But from the position of his third eye, there was a sort of tail which was white and hung down to the floor. I cannot explain any more than this or what the dream meant, but I wonder if he is living with me in another dimension; maybe one day I will know.

Stuck in a Vortex

Several nights running, I awoke from sound sleep and spent the following days feeling exhausted as a result of sensing someone whispering in my ear, tugging the bed covers, blowing in my face, or tapping my arm. I consulted spiritual books that told me to pray to Archangel Michael for the release of these energies. I tried psychics from a well-known college in London, and they told me they could get rid of the spirits waking me up if I gave them 400 pounds! I also spoke to my guides many times. They told me to be nice to the spirits and ask if they could see a light ahead of them and then suggest that it would be beneficial for them to go there and not hang around the earthly plane. But none of this worked, and each night was the same.

I blamed myself for things like eating too much before bedtime or having inadvertently been amongst other low-life characters in doubtful areas of London pubs, but in the end, I just gave up. When I did try speaking to these spirits, I found out that a middle-aged man had murdered his wife's lover; another was a younger man who had been stabbed locally and woke up on the other side; and the third wanted to help me but pestered me with his non-stop chattering that made no sense whatsoever, so I decided he must have been a bit deranged when he passed over.

Another Helpful Suggestion

This suggestion for how to solve the problem came from an expert on astral travel. He asked me, "Do you see a vortex?" I replied yes immediately. He explained, "You have to imagine each spirit, if you see it or just imagine it; send it up through the vortex, into the atmosphere, and out into space, and it won't bother you again." Needless to say, that didn't work either. Before the survey mentioned previously, a spirit called Peter said that the house was built on ley lines, and there was a time many years before when there were no houses there at all. The area was a place where people came to heal their spirit, as they were aware of an underground city, as Peter called it. He told me that the spirits hanging around could go to the light and return whenever they wanted to, and unfortunately for me, they seemed to derive pleasure in keeping me awake! This went on for months, and through this time, I did not want to write anything or do any exercise; in fact, anything creative came to a standstill. My guardian angel told me not to talk with the spirits or have anything to do with them. This was difficult, and sometimes I wanted to help them move on.

Coming home from holidays, we would be met by rooms that were full of not only stale air but also a disgusting smell. Flinging open windows and spraying air freshener was a short-term solution.

When I saw a white light in my third eye or in the room, I knew it was a good spirit, angel, or guide present; when I saw a dark spot, I knew it was a bad spirit. I sent the dark spirits through the vortex and pray for it to go to God, the angels, and light – to a better place away from the darkness where it existed. At first, these bad spirits returned to boast that no matter how many times I asked them to go to the light, they could and would return if they wanted to.

What finally worked was a combination of praying to Archangel Michael, Raphael, Uriel, and Gabriel again, requesting their assistance; using wax earplugs, which blocked out the chatter to a degree; and turning on an air purifier (because bad spirits nearly always bring bad smells with them). I also chanted, "Om mani padme hum," over and over, which helped the bad spirits go away. It was also important to be kind to myself, be positive, and stay focused on the task at hand.

Peter, the kind spirit, returned on a couple of occasions. He said, "Sorry for disturbing you. I will let you sleep, but thank you for helping us all move on."

For some people, having an angel-card reading and using a clear quartz pendulum to detect which chakras are blocked does the trick; this can point you in the right direction to clear the block for good. If a chakra is blocked and you still feel the effects, it is probably a part of your life purpose to work your way through the situation as a life lesson to grow spiritually.

Angels of Atlantis

There has much been written on this subject, but I find the deck of Atlantis angel cards to be invaluable. Recently, when I needed to feel uplifted, I pulled the following cards:

Sandolphin
Many changes are occurring now. Chant "haw." This will help you ground yourself as you move through the cycle of change and incorporate the many changes.

Jophiel
"Hah" chanted three times through the heart energy centre helps liberate you from any challenge with discernment.

Michael
Chant "hee" three times through the crown energy centre; this resonates with connection of enchantment.

Hanael
Chant, "Om namah shivaya," three times; the divine illuminates the way forward.

These words couldn't have been more fitting to what I was experiencing at the time.

Energy Is Simply Energy

Experts on this subject say that energy is simply energy. When it has the same inception and vibrates with the same consistency, it easily gravitates to familiar territory. The connection blends together, recreating the environment from which both energies were formed. So what goes on over London? Could the Olympics have created all this action in the sky above us? Or is it a sign of the development of a higher purpose taking place and the lower energies resisting and rising up? The latter, I think, is the simpler explanation, as we know that 2012 brought about such a rise in vibration for our planet that will bring about good energies ultimately. However, I would be interested to hear further explanations.

But we humans are much more than simply energy. Our spiritual guides and masters repeatedly tell us that our minds are far greater than we imagine. We can sail the oceans, fly the skies, and invent wonderful masterpieces, computers, rockets, architecture, health cures, and so on. And we are capable of using much more than our minds.

Trance Healing

I have attempted to stretch my mind in different spiritual directions, and trance healing was one of these ways. After attending some trance healing sessions, which involved receiving information and manifesting in my third eye, I began to question the truth and accuracy of the information a recipient receives. This uncertainty was answered when I was shown, at the end of a long meditation, the image of a Christlike figure with arms that became wings raised above his head, motioning towards the person to whom I was sending thoughts and requests of healing. This person was on a chair in front of me, with his back to me. The manifestation was real enough to me, but the healing itself was a feeling that the healing was taking place. The recipient confirmed afterwards that he felt wonderfully healed and uplifted.

My trance healing partner and I are proof that energy can be and is regularly transferred and channelled simultaneously with the exchange of our energies whilst engaging in thought processes. Complicated, yes, but also wonderful when you think about it in such depth.

I look forward to the day when more and more people, on a worldwide scale, become aware and engage regularly in such exchanges of energy for the highest good of all!

Elementals

After first noticing faces in trees locally and elsewhere in the countryside, I kept seeing bearded wise men, an owl, and dogs.

With the fifth-dimensional change that came about after December 2012, this has steadily developed. I have seen odd characters such as Nemus, who appeared on a tree trunk in our garden that we were trying to destroy.

The tree had grown roots and spread underneath the lawn in many places, but after we killed the new roots in spring 2013, the tree unbelievably began to sprout new leaves. People who study angels call this particular tree the Tree of Heaven, perhaps because you cannot stop it from growing!

One day, I was looking out the window and saw the smiling face of what looked like a gnome on the trunk of this tree; it looked as if somebody had carved him there. His smile went from ear to ear, and he had (and still has) a beard, twinkling eyes, and a longish nose. Above him, a female face with pointed ears recently appeared, looking a bit like Disney's fairy Tinker Bell. She spoke to me in my mind and said that her name was Ceniti. It was a very unusual name, I thought, but she explained that she and the gnome figure came to save the tree that we were trying to destroy. She has not appeared since, so perhaps if we leave the tree to thrive, the elementals will be happy. I can agree to that as long as the tree confines its roots to one area.

Ceniti is the nearest I have come to seeing a fairy, although a very experienced medium friend of mine, Lorraine Heron, told me I had a fairy with me over ten years ago. Sometimes I hear a tinkling sound, and my fairy friend announces herself as Esme, perhaps bringing a bit of magic into my life. She comes and goes like most elementals, as they have a job to do in looking after our plant life. Even more recently, a female appeared in the same tree with wide eyes and a lovely smile. Nemus said she is his wife, Delphine, named after the flower. I thanked them and look forward to her help with the garden flowers.

Various faces of elementals have appeared amongst the leaves in the bushes and trees, looking half-human, half-animal, with pointy ears and pug noses and puppy-dog eyes. Many people who are clairvoyant and clairsentient around this world can see and hear the same sorts of things I do and more. And this is on the increase, as many spiritualists have opened their third eyes even further since the vibrations of our planet have risen since December 2012.

The Winter Garden

A little bird among the trees
Shivers with the gentle breeze
As tawny owl takes sudden flight,
Swoops on supper for the night.

The moon above, in fulsome glow,
Lighting up the world below.
As snow on ice would gently glisten,
Wide-eyed vision, deftly listen.

For all that's live with midnight air
Would stop to look with stealthy stare
And then pounce on prey to satisfy
Their hungry lust on passer-by.

While sleeping humans miss the show,
The actors scurry to and fro.
This is life the way goes on
Till morning birds awake with song.

Unicorns

Alphedia works closely with unicorns. I've had experience with these creatures on and off over the years. I see what I call a divine spark in my third eye, a bright-white light that appears when I meditate or practise Reiki. But some people call this a unicorn. Some experts on the angelic spheres say that when a unicorn is close to us, the spark is at its weakest; when the spark is very bright, is the creature is a long distance away. Other spiritual experts say that the spark of light we see is our strongest, most direct link with the source of creativity, or God.

The unicorns (which I see as a twinkling light or sometimes as white horses with horns on their forehead) are here to help raise our consciousness levels, so don't be afraid or alarmed if you see any; just be welcoming. Alphedia says that she often sees one or two before retiring for the night, similar to my experience.

A few years ago, I saw in my third eye several showers of what would describe as sparkling, twinkling stars. It felt as if they were being thrown at me! The bursts made me smile and gave me a good feeling. Even now, I remember those few moments of pow, pow, pow as they came into my vision in quick succession. It was a wonderful experience.

When I began meditating directly with the unicorns, I met my guardian unicorn, Greta, and she told me that I had been communicating with them for some time. I believed her, as I am not always given names or visual presences when I communicate with beings in other dimensions.

I learned that the unicorns have a hierarchy. There are royal unicorns at the head of each group who decide what frequencies will be brought down to our planet. They reside in the seventh dimension, where archangels and ascended masters also exist. Regal leader unicorns are more detached than elemental unicorns and guardian unicorns; their energy is more attuned to the physical realm, and they reside in the individual's aura.

Royalty unicorns are available now for lightworkers who have been working hard to raise their vibrations in their meditations. They help change your physical structure to a more crystalline structure.

Romance Unicorns

To communicate with romance unicorns, sit in your heart centre (leave negativity, ego, and unworthiness behind), and in pure-mindedness, clear your heart and feel your emotions of higher vibrations (where gratitude, honesty, and romantic love can be found). You can buy flowers for yourself to emanate romance and draw romance and love to you. Romance is a divine state of being.

Elemental Unicorns

The vibration of elemental unicorns is closest in a native birch forest. I saw many unicorn orbs in such a forest when I stayed close to one in Kent last Easter. When they allow you to connect with them, carry a rose quartz to help you align your energy with pure love. They are shy, so this helps show that your heart is pure and that you are working for the highest good. Meditate on the intent of your heart centre.

Guardian Unicorns

Guardian unicorns are here to help us on our divine life path and may travel with your guardian angel. My guardian unicorn, Greta, and my guardian angel, Sheba, come to me together when I meditate. This type of unicorn reconnects us with pure love and reminds us that we are all love.

You may have more than one Guardian unicorn travelling with you in your aura. When you are ready, try to communicate with this being that can bring you spiritual guidance and help and a connection with the world of pure love and divine energy.

The Difference between Angels and Fairies

Fairies are beings of nature, part of this world although they exist in a different dimension.

Angels are divine beings and messengers from God. They exist in a different astral plane but are coming to earth to help earth and its inhabitants ascend.

Body Elementals

I learned recently about the body elemental that is with us from the day we are born, throughout our entire life. I contacted my body elemental recently by sitting in a quiet place, breathing in and out to gently raise my energy thoughts, and then giving thanks to my body elemental for helping relieve the tension headache that I had. Shortly afterwards, I realized the pain had gone. I thanked my body elemental for helping me, adding that I was very grateful, as I could get on with my work. Just say in your mind or out loud, "Body elemental, please can you remove the pain from such and such an area," and don't be surprised if the pain goes away soon. Don't try this for any serious condition that you are taking regular medication for, but it is well worth asking for achy limbs or muscle pain. You don't have to know the elemental's name. Always say thank you, as it loves you to show appreciation. Your body elemental is separate from your aura. It is a part of your brain energy that you connect to.

AFFIRMATION

I see beyond any difficulties before me, knowing that my guardian angel helps me retain my spiritual values.

CHAPTER 9

Contact with Guides

The best method of connecting with our guides in spirit is through meditation, contemplation, and prayer. This brings spirit energy close to us, enabling awareness of its presence working in our lives. It is necessary, though, to value our inner capacity to access the spirit.

We may know our main guide from another lifetime, but its role is to assist us in being true to our intentions in this lifetime and to protect our psychic space. It does this by being available at our inner level of vibration. Whatever level of spirit knowledge we gain, it is important that we are sincere and reach the truth in our hearts.

Through the help of our personal guides, we learn to face our inner truth and deal with the trials that we, as souls, have set for ourselves. Fear, guilt, shame, resentment, anger, or despair can distract us from loving and helping others along their path towards achieving their life purpose.

By training ourselves to become inwardly alert and accept help from our spiritual sources, we can choose positive thoughts to guide our everyday lives. As we become successful in living out our soul plan and our spiritual guides help us appropriately, they will be able to move further along their own paths.

By taking responsibility for what we think, our outer circumstances might also change, and opportunities could come to us that we did not anticipate. This is a learning process for our guides as well as us. Nothing is set, and even plans made on high spiritual planes can be affected by choices of individuals.

Where We Go When We Pass to Spirit

There is a place that exists on the closest plane to earth, and it is much more beautiful than our plane. Solid matter such as we have on earth e.g. trees, fields, mountains even water will been seen in a more fluid way. But love is the prevailing emotion we will experience there.

Our soul vibrations would need to be raised to a higher level for us to experience the various other planes that exist. These realms are for us to further our learning on the many other planes in the spirit world. Our guides explain that some of these are called the halls of learning, where we can choose to study any subject we wish. We may go to the halls of memories to be alone, with perhaps only our guide to accompany us; we will be confronted with our actions, thoughts, and feelings from our most recent lifetime and confront the effects we had on others. In the halls of healing, our soul may receive healing from other souls, and we may learn to specialise in this area ourselves. In addition, there are levels where we may be creative through music and art forms. We may meet up with our loved ones at any time should we wish, and we will learn how to connect with our soul brothers and sisters. There are many, many books written on these topics in much more detail than I have gone into here.

AFFIRMATION

I quieten my mind and connect through the stillness and silence within me to the vibration of my guides in spirit.

CHAPTER 10

Life between Lives Session with Paul Williamson

My Own Experience

Many people do not understand past-life regression sessions and may be scared of them, but I felt perfectly comfortable and at ease whenever I am regressed back to previous lifetimes of my own.. Each time, I was fully aware of my present physical life whilst speaking about my past life. It was obvious to me that I had accessed a different dimension of my soul energy.

This particular session was with well-known author Paul Williamson, who has written six books on the subject. I was first regressed back to one of my lives in which I was a male called Richard.

P: "You are walking down ten steps, and there is a door in front of you; can you describe it?"

C: "It's a large door, round at the top, with a big heavy circular handle, and there are studs in the door. I have to push to open it."

P: "You are inside now. What do you see?"

C: "I see steps going down. There is a lawn and flowers, and I am standing on gravel in soft, suede-type shoes. I have a red jacket on that is edged with gold, and it has big turnback cuffs on the arms that are yellow. I am a male adult."

P: "Are you alone?"

C: "No, I am with my lady. She has a pale-blue long dress with flowers in her hair. She carries a fan and has ringlets in her hair. I am close to her; I sweep down and bow to her, and I feel happy and smile at her. She takes my arm, and we walk around the gardens. They are my gardens, and I feel pride."

P: "Can you describe the building?"

C: "It is square with big windows. We are eating in the dining room, which has wooden panels. There is a long table with high-backed chairs, and it's just my lady friend with me; we are being served a meal by servants, who are carrying the food on silver plates with silver lids."

P: "Can you describe a typical day?"

C: "I go to the stable, as I breed horses. I go over the household accounts; there are ten people in the house, and six of these have to be checked. The village people come to me with their problems, and I help people with money and advice. I go to church on Sundays and offer them spiritual advice and counselling."

P: "Please describe one of the villagers who came to you for advice."

C: "One of them had a pig stolen." [I laugh.] "There is no authority around to help them, and I give him a few shillings. I advise him to secure the pig pens and get more security around him and that he should get a dog as a warning."

P: "Describe a get-together."

C: "There is a maypole up for children, and everyone is happy. There is a violin playing and people dancing to the music. The local townspeople, priest, and vicar are there. There is not much nobility, as it's a local fair. I am watching the festivities now."

P: "Can you describe an official occasion?"

C: "Yes, I am in the village hall, in a meeting to build a proper road, and it will need a lot of money. It's another's idea, and we talk of the supply of labour and money."

P: "Can you describe an emergency situation in your life?"

C: "Yes, we are outside in a horse-drawn carriage being held up by highwaymen, and we are made to get outside the carriage. I am with my lady friend; we decide not to resist. We hand over our money, and my lady friend gives her jewellery over. We are tied up but remain calm."

P: "Can you tell me about a special occasion?"

C: "We are at a big wedding in London in a big church; there are many people there, all dressed up. I am in the front row; I am uncle to the girl who is being married, and I am wearing a wig. I enjoy the wedding with its wonderful pomp and pageantry. There are friends and family there."

P: "What is your name?"

C: "I am Richard, and my lady friend is Anne."

P: "Can you describe your most proud official moment?"

C: "I am given a medal from the king for loyalty to the Crown, and I am very proud."

P: "Describe your death."

C: "I am inside the house, in my sixties, in a four-poster bed. I am coughing; it's pneumonia. My lady is there. I just let go, and it's a relief."

P: "What is the year?"

C: "The year is 1724."

Paul continued, leading me to another life that presented itself at the same session. This time, I was living at the time of Christ, and my name was John.

P: "Describe the door in front of you."

C: "It's a black door with no handle, and I push it open. Someone is reading from a big book; I feel I am in a church. The sun is shining through the window with no glass in it. I wear long robes, and the people are bending in prayer. Soldiers come bursting in through the main door, and everyone looks around at them."

P: "Describe what the people are wearing."

C: "Long white robes. The soldiers are taking me out, and they are being very rough. I am male. They push me to the floor, and

I get up. They are marching me down the road while people are throwing things at the soldiers, anything they can lay their hands on. They put me in a cell of bare stone. I look around and realize that I cannot do any writing and feel very alone."

P: "What do you do in this lifetime?"

C: "I support Jesus. I spread news about him, and I do lots of writing. I am a preacher."

Preaching

P: "What do you see?"

C: "People, crowds of people, out in the streets; they are disciples of Jesus, giving bread to the people. Jesus brings truth about God: a new life is promised, a better life."

With Jesus

C: "He talks, and I am writing about what we should do next. We are discussing the next meeting – where it's to be and how to get the word around. Jesus has long brown wavy hair, he wears white robes, and he is wonderful. I feel honoured to be with him. He is doing good. He is really needed, and there is no one like him. He is gentle and kind."

Inside

P: "Back to your passing – describe it."

C: "There is a woman there like a nun; she is wiping my forehead. I have grey hair; I am not eating. I am pleased with my lifetime."

P: "You are passing now. Can you describe it?"

C: "I am floating upwards. I see only colours. I feel relaxed. I am meeting Jesus's soul. I see him before me, and I drop to my knees. I have my arms around his legs, and I begin to cry with happiness. I stand up and we hug."

Between Paul's questions and each time we moved to another place, there was usually a short while during which I was asked to breathe in. At these times, I drifted on to the place he asked me to go. I felt totally safe and protected by the two angel energies placed alongside me.

P: "We are going back to your childhood in this lifetime. You see the front door of where you lived at the age of twelve; can you describe it?"

C: "I see a plain door in front of me, and as I go through it, I am in a living room. I am going to my bedroom, the second room on the left down the hallway. Inside, there is a bed with a pink cover on it, a wardrobe, and a record player."

P: "You are now outside your home, and you are seven years old; what are you wearing, and what are you doing?"

C: "I am skipping, with a friend of mine holding the rope at one end and another friend holding the rope at the other end. I am wearing my favourite skirt; it's a blue tartan kilt, and I am happy."

P: "We are going back now to your earliest memory, when you were two years old; where are you, and what are you doing?"

C: "I am outside in the backyard. My brothers are there, and I am watching them play. It's a warm day. I am sat down watching them play, and I am eating biscuits. I am wearing a ribbon in my hair."

P: "You are now going back to when you were in your mother's womb; how do you feel, and what do you sense?"

I began to feel a bit cold and shaky. Paul explained afterwards that the body can react in this way to express slight fear of going back to an unknown time or place.

C: "I feel warm and have space to move around. I hear a noise, children squealing; they are close by, and I feel I want to get out and join in! I can hear my mother's heartbeat, and it is comforting. I feel love from her, and she seems nice."

P: "We are going back to the time when you were in spirit, finally going to inhabit a body; how do you feel?"

C: "I feel weird – it's restrictive."

P: "Is it interesting to work with this body?"

C: "It's a sense of wholeness; this body is going to be complete in its journey, it's a good match."

We went to a place to meet a guide or another presence. I felt myself travelling through time. I saw tiny bright lights falling away on either side of me. A being called Jenna joined me. I felt her very close to me; she was golden, with golden hair, and I got a very good feeling from her. Jenna told me she was my guide and then gave me the following message:

> "Life will be a struggle, but your journey will be complete; each step will bring you closer to your creator. Help will come whenever you need it – just ask. Wise ones will surround you with love, understanding, and peace, and you will prosper."

C: "I see a light above me, a golden light, and a presence."

This was a wonderful experience for me, as I saw a hand appear, and it stroked my hand very gently and said, "God loves you."

Paul now asks what I can see, and I say it's God's divine spark of light rising upwards and disappearing from view of my third eye.

Most Recent Past Life

When I was regressed to my most recent life the session followed much the same questioning as before i.e. where I was standing and what was I wearing. So for ease of reading and the avoidance of unnecessary repetition I have left out all the obvious questions for this session and only included the answers.

C: "I have coal beneath my feet, and I am walking up a slag heap. I am outside, and I am not cold or hot. I am wearing lace-up boots, a cap on my head, and an apron over a long dress. I am five years old, and I can clearly see myself at the top of the heap. I am with a young boy. I begin smiling and feel happy; we are enjoying ourselves, getting dirty."

C: "I am at home now in a terraced cottage, eating in the kitchen. My dad is there; he has a black moustache and a big cap like a Geordie. My mum is quite slim and at the stove; she is kind. There is my baby brother in a wooden cradle on the floor. My name is Pam, and I am the eldest. I go to a small school. There are ten children in the class, and we sit at wooden desks. The teacher is writing on the blackboard." [I break into a giggle.] "We call her Miss Prim. I do enjoy school."

C: "I am now in a church being married, wearing a long dress with small frills around the shoulder. He has got a brown suit on; there are twenty people there. I love him, and he's kind. There is a plain gold ring on my finger and we kiss. We walk down the aisle, smiling and happy. My cousins are there and my mum and dad. My husband's name is John, and he only has his mum, sister, and friends there."

C: "I am a housewife in my married life. He has just come home from his job, and I have cooked dinner; we have no children and we are happy together, though we still yearn for children."

C: "I have two sons now. I am giving birth to one of my children; there is a midwife there, and she hands the baby to me; this is my eldest son, John Junior."

C: "My greatest fulfilment in this life is having grandchildren. The family is going on, and John is still with me. There have been challenges in making ends meet, but I have stayed calm."

C: "I am feeling weak now. I am sixty-five. I am in my own bed with my family there. I am thinking of the struggles that we have overcome. I am told that all the struggles will be overcome. There is a vicar there, wearing glasses; he's saying a prayer for my soul."

The Passing

C: "I see myself above my body, feeling relief. My death was necessary. I am floating upwards; there is a line or a kind of rope going upwards, and the space gets light. I am travelling – small lights are fading away into the distance. I can sense the movement as I am still travelling. Something is coming on my right; there are streams of light opening to the spirit world. I need healing. There is a healing light coming in; it's my soul. I see pink, purple, and green and feel relaxed."

My Guide

"We are in your consciousness; we communicate with you telepathically. Your soul was enslaved; your heart was at peace every step of the way. Discoveries are yet to come."

My Soul Speaks Now

"If you keep on this path, it will lead to satisfaction of your soul. Your achievements thus far have satisfied your heart, mind, and soul. Extra healing is coming to you. So, to receive it, you must continue to ask if this is the way it is going to be. Ascended masters surround your work. Keep on keeping on, as White Eagle says. Discoveries are yet to be revealed. Keep knocking on every door. Discoveries are yet to be unfolded. You'll be safe under your own umbrella."

My Spiritual Name

"I am being told that my spiritual name is Estrellar."

The Wise Council Speaks

"I need to study meditation areas, to access higher help – increased senses; help will come.

What of Completion?

"Each soul has a lifetime to discover its true potential; this incarnation will complete its potential. The discoveries are essential as you progress on this path. There are many here ready to help you."

My Spirit Mother Guide

"Her name is Jenna; she visits me. She is part of the wise council.

Paul then asks me what my specialisation in the spirit world is, and

> I reply, "I am a galactic traveller who has come to earth. I have been to other worlds, and I am here to serve and to guide others forward to the golden age. I am part of a group in spirit 10,000 strong: lightworkers who guide humanity forward.
>
> "In my soul group, I teach spiritually. I am good at teaching on a basic soul level – teaching beginner souls. I am in what looks like a classroom; we are in a circle. I teach seven beings, and each one has connections with incarnates; they are teacher souls. I am teaching them from my experience in my incarnations. They are learning to be guides, experience existence as guides."

Paul asks me why I am here at this time:

> "This is a special time on earth; many want to be here at this time, even the teacher souls. With the seven souls, I am teaching them how to blend their imprints with incarnates – for the incarnates to learn more spiritually – and to bring thoughts into their mind. How to keep their hearts pure and incarnates' thoughts pure. Incarnates need to be guided and need to be open and willing, and those wanting to learn make progress. For those incarnates who are not open, that is their decision; they are beyond remit."

Paul asks me to describe the meeting with the 10,000 lightworkers.

> "There are groups within groups, and they amass in the golden temple. The groups are together, and the wise council speaks about plans and of the different levels to be achieved; that's the main function. Each group

has an old soul to help guide the others, the ones I know in incarnation; there are those I recognize, like an affiliation. I set them to achieve. It is more fluid than it sounds, as there is no strict timeline, just goals. Earth-conscious humanity and peace at the moment is the main goal; it's going slowly but coming about."

Paul asks me to describe planning my incarnation, but I only say the following:

"Love is around me like a capsule, an etheric capsule, I'm in. I see colours."

And he asks what I have learned.

"I am glad I got into the council to confirm what I am lacking in and that I am going to receive help."

My Chinese guide appears:

"I hear him. It's Kim. He says he thought I would never ask him to speak. He says, "You know, Christine, I would never abandon you. I will always help with your readings. You have much work to do; let's speak again when you are ready. You know we have a clear channel."

I am smiling and happy, as I have gotten to know Kim very well over the years.

AFFIRMATION

I meditate through my heart and mind where clarity, discernment and truth exists within my soul.

CHAPTER 11

Ascended Master Messages

Lord Melchizedek

Lord Melchizedek Is an ascended master, who is known as the father of all initiates. He lived in the time of Atlantis and Lemuria, the ancient cities where people's lives were steeped in the awesome power and knowledge of spirit that transcended their existence on earth. He comes to us in dreams and meditations as the energy for lightworkers. Invoking the essence of Lord Melchizedek's energy can bring about changes of consciousness and awareness that realign our physical and spiritual bodies for the highest good of all. All we have to do is ask his permission.His message is: "Be positive and assertive in your ventures, and your lives will become more enjoyable as you grow in wisdom along the way.

St Germain

I was sitting at my laptop reading a message about St Germain by the prophet Elizabeth Clare, when I felt a flood of energy in my right arm and received the name of St Germain in my mind, and then I received the following message:

"Yes, you have connected to St Germain, as you were reading my words via Elizabeth, who is now with us. You and I connect through the violet flame and also the embodiment of Paul Veronese.

"What is about to happen in America is applicable to Europe; the United Kingdom is adjusting the style of governing towards the ordinary person, exercising their freedom of creativity: to be compensated in their share of a more just reward. A gradual realization is taking place, as we speak, that democracy and exploitation of workers belongs in the past. Cooperation will bring about a dissemination of the hierarchy structure. With this will come an acceleration of the individuals who have been kept down by the control of large corporations who, through greed and selfishness, have remained in power.

"So, power shifting will bring satisfaction in individuals on a soul level as their higher self is rewarded and given a reason to express themselves in the way God desires."

The message ended with, "Seek God first; the violet flame will connect you."

As I have been working with the violet flame for a few years now, I knew exactly what this meant. Calling upon the violet ray in meditation can bring about an inner uplifting, spiritual knowledge, spiritual wisdom, and necessary shifts of higher consciousness to bring about change on all levels of our lives. It is also the colour of energy that can transmute negativity or stuck energy within ourselves or our homes or workplaces.

Message to Estrellar

God gave me the cosmic name Estrellar; since this happened, messages are channelled to me at special times (one of these is published below). This name (which is also the name of a star) was confirmed to me during my most recent life between lives regression session with Paul Williamson.

In the following message, the archangel Michael spoke of a time in the future when wars have ceased and the golden age is born. I found his words incredibly inspirational and full of hope for earthlings, showing that if we change our hearts and minds, our souls will be affected by our thoughts, words, and deeds. In time, we will create a new golden age.

Message channelled from Archangel Michael on 11.11.11

To Estrellar and You

> When wars amongst men have ceased and peace rules the earth, the golden age will be born. When every man, woman, and child stands in wonder at God's creation — the flowers, the birds, the trees, the clouds, the rivers, the streams, the fish, the oceans, and all of nature – peace will dwell in your hearts again.
>
> The dynamic force of the universe and its creative energies affecting earth will bring an end to greed and avarice; harmony and balance will follow. Heart, mind, body, and soul will come together as nations recognize this need; their peoples will be inspired to raise their consciousness levels, for goodness and goodwill to be not just a dream but a reality.
>
> Angels, masters and guides have been working overtime to bring all this to the earth and its inhabitants, as God's words have not been heeded. Healing energies from the heavenly hosts are now beaming love to those who witness the effects of spiritual values and pass on energies and messages such as this for the good of all mankind.

I ask you to heed these words and look deep in your heart to see what changes your consciousness can bring to your life as caring thoughts touch others. No good deed goes unmissed in your soul. First, seek God in your thoughts, words, and deeds; your life, your family's life, and your neighbour's life will change for the good of all.

I am a follower of the White Eagle movement, a worldwide organisation. From time to time, I receive inspiring messages such as the following one, which are sent to help and guide all of us spiritually.

One of the primary lessons is that of discrimination between the false and the true, the real and the unreal, and right and wrong. No one can teach us; no one can give us this divine attribute of discrimination ... You have to see things from a truer perspective. You have to develop discernment – discrimination between what is worthwhile and what is worthless. You have to choose the better way.

The better way has to become a living reality for us, not because of what we are told, but because it is what we want.

Messengers from our world come with tender love – not to carry your burdens or rob you of the opportunities to develop your character. They come to bring you love and to help you to see light, not to take away your responsibilities. So, it is your affair to decide your own material acts. Do not throw your responsibilities or your karma onto your loving guides.

Spirit communicators will not mislead; they will convey simplicity, humility, love, and inspiration and teach the truths of life. Always, however, beware of any message that says, "Do this; do that. Go here; go there." No one has the right to say to another, "You must" or "You should not." The decision rests entirely with the individual.

White Eagle on Discrimination and Discernment

Through Pain and Suffering

Pain and suffering may be inflicted by one soul upon many, but you are astonished to see that what appeared to be evil was in reality a power set in motion to bring about knowledge and good, to give people a power of selection, discernment, and discrimination.

Through Tolerance

Remember that all the qualities of the soul are manifested through the physical man or woman according to that person's degree of evolution. For instance, in the younger soul, the quality of love manifests itself through violent or childish passions, uncontrolled and undisciplined. It has to be trained and directed to the highest point of aspiration. When someone is manifesting at their lowest level which is a place of extreme negativity, they can cause pain and suffering in their own physical and emotional body. But by slow degrees, through experiencing pain and suffering, the being understands the wisdom of applying this love and emotion in the right way. In the beginning, the lesson is learnt through discretion, discrimination, and most of all tolerance. If you can be tolerant towards humanity – towards individuals – you are taking a big step forward upon the path of discipline and the unfolding of your higher self.

St Michael's Day Message

To Estrellar and You

On 29 September 2013, I received this special message from the archangel Michael on the subject of the golden age.

> Many millions of people are seeking my channellings at this exact time. Regarding the current movement of the spiritual advancement of mankind, we are witnessing a change of some magnitude. Many people are passing to spirit by different means; this will increase, and devastations will come about.
>
> By 2014 a different world order will come into effect, or at the least it will have commenced and grown. Little things in the hearts and minds of man and governance have changed and will continue to do so, moving more rapidly over the coming months and years.
>
> Peace will be a priority, followed by the pursuit of fairness and establishing a more just society. We are all working towards this objective by inspiring lightworkers, individually and collectively, towards completion in the 2030s.
>
> Chosen ones have willingly offered their help to bring these necessary changes. Volunteers amongst the angel hierarchy and galactic realms are being led by the wise counsel to achieve a new earth.

I asked Michael this question, "Once this order has been established, will Jesus or other masters return to guide incarnates?"

He replied, "It has not actually happened yet in your time, but masters are with you. There is more and more need for humans to connect spiritually with their inner guidance. This is the way forward. Masters will reincarnate to maintain the status quo. Believe, trust, and have faith; all will be revealed in time. Blessings."

The Ancient Mystery Schools

The following text is an extract from Spiritual Unfoldment Three, *published by The White Eagle Publishing Trust.*

Ages ago, when the present human cycle was in the process of birth, wise beings, those we call God-men and God-women, came to this planet from worlds which had already evolved far beyond any spiritual growth conceivable by yourselves. These beings brought knowledge of the ancient mysteries to the earth: they came here to establish schools of wisdom for the guidance of humankind. Temples were built wherein those who were ready were received, instructed and learned of the mysteries of life, the ancient wisdom.

Note: White Eagle often speaks in very old fashioned terminology.

They were taught from the invisible worlds also. Remember: all that manifests on earth is first born from the invisible and comes through later into physical or outer manifestation. So in these schools of learning or of light, the mysteries of life, even before they were manifest on earth, were studied in reverence and awe.

To this day, in the secret places of the earth, tablets of stone can be found upon which this ancient knowledge is inscribed in symbol; relics hidden in the mountains, in caves or temples. Such records are also imprinted on the ether, and are called the etheric or akashic records, to be read only by initiates, those who are ready.

Today all are free to seek the mysteries. Once a man or a woman longs for wisdom, not out of curiosity, or to satisfy a greedy mind, or for his or her own satisfaction, but rather that he or she may serve, then they set their feet upon a path which leads ultimately to enlightenment. When a soul through this great longing and searching finds his or her path, then teaching and guidance come from the invisible. Having found his or her path, the soul should remain true to it, be true to the inner light. We suggest following the one, avoiding the many;, be true to your inner light: and the mysteries of the invisible worlds will be revealed to you in the degree that you are ready and will use the knowledge thus attained in selfless service. And remember, service can take many forms. You are not bound to this or that particular form of service, but you should obey the guidance of your heart.

AFFIRMATION

I can help the needs of those around me by keeping my eyes, ears, and heart open.

CHAPTER 12

Conversations with God

G always speaks to me lovingly and takes care that what he says is on my level of understanding. The main reason I publish my conversations with him is to inspire you to take the bold step towards developing your own spirituality; it has many different paths to unfolding in your life. I appreciate that some readers will have had similar experiences, but everyone has a unique story to tell.

Who Created Us?

To find the authentic answer on the subject of who created us, I turned to the highest source that I know, G. Many people ask me, "Who is our creator, and is it true there is only one God?"

I am told that there are many other universes and many other gods who created them, but this is a vast subject. To this day, despite all the so-called experts on the subject, we can only rely on channellings from spirits in the hierarchies that surround us and the odd glimpses of the other side that those fortunate enough to be clairvoyant witness.

I accept the theory that there is an ultimate God or creator of our life-force energy in our universe, and there are two supreme knowledgeable beings below him, her, or it that pass their spiritual knowledge and power down to the archangels and angels. On another level are the entities, and below that level are humans. So, there are families of spiritual knowledge, truth, and power we can access to pass it on to others to live honest lives. We can only try to help show the way forwards and must leave it to the powers that be to create the miracles from a higher level as they see fit to influence life for the good of all.

I leave it up to you to decide as to the authenticity of my conversations with G, as reproduced here.

C: "Is it true that angels never speak with each other?"

G: "They communicate with enormous energy and incredibly strong intuition, and they have the powerful ability to manipulate energy around humans for the good of mankind. This is what I created them for. Does this answer your question?"

C: "Yes, for the moment. Thank you. Why do they not smile or change their expressions?"

G: "This is not true. As you have read in Lorna Byrne's books, the angels do smile and show expression."

I then asked G about communicating with Peter and Harry, two entities who had been speaking to me recently.

C: "These two spirits have come to me, and they are difficult to hear sometimes. Why is this?"

G: "You know the answer to this: the depth of the force field (energy) ether that exists around you at any given time is variable, making communication easier or harder at times."

C: "Will humans one day develop a method, such as a telephone, to talk more clearly with the spirit world?"

G: "That invention would bring a loss of freedom for spirits to retain their higher dimensional existence as whole entities. The potential would arise for the human soul to be bombarded" – I felt G smile at this word – "with many aspects of lifetimes at once, checking to see how each life is panning out at any given time or space."

C: "I never thought of it that way. Maybe it's not a good idea then. But surely with mediums and psychics this does take place already – albeit on a lesser scale."

G: "Yes, but that scale is something like 5 per cent of the worldwide populous."

C: "Why is this?"

G: "This ability has not always reached humans who can develop this part of their spirituality. The potential is there in most people, but through stubbornness or a lack of seeking to use their mind or soul, it remains dormant in the majority."

C: "Will this change in 2013?"

G: "Indeed it will. The higher dimensions are using all of their influence towards this vision for future generations in the golden age to come. Bless you."

I then asked G about dual or triple lifetimes (with each life belonging to one soul).

C: "I know you have discussed this before, but the question comes up a lot. Is it possible to live one lifetime incarnated on earth and be living another lifetime, say in the future or the past, at exactly the same time? This is based on your statement that there is no time, as everything takes place at the same time."

G: "We have covered this before. Yes, it is possible to have more than two lives at one time, based on the truth that everything takes place at the same time in spirit. Bless you in your work."

G then gave me the following poem:

The way may not always be clear.
The future may not always appear.
When you want to see like a seer,
Trust and believe I will remove your fear.

Past-Life Regression

C: "What are you views on past-life regression, please? I understand that this exercise can release blocks that exist in someone's present life from a previous one."

G: "As you were thinking, it is not necessarily something anyone can handle or would be ready to deal with."

C: "Can you give me a scenario?"

G: "Of course. A teenage male experiencing many changes on an emotional level, without having developed his spiritual side, could be plunged into a past life that's devastating for him to experience again, albeit on a soul level."

C: "But surely the hypnotherapist would take precautions to ensure the young man went back to a life with a good experience?"

G: "Again, this is not so. The soul will usually take the recipient to a life that teaches the boy a lesson he did not learn in the past. But you know all this!"

C: "I wanted to hear it from you. I also think, of course, this exercise would not help a mentally disturbed person."

G: "It depends on the cause of the mental disturbance. If the person went through a given experience in his or her present life, it could be helpful to experience this at a soul level when he or she overcame such experiences."

Earth-Bound Spirits

C: "Why are some spirits allowed to return to earth and annoy people in their own homes?"

G: "Ah! In general, very few spirits return to certain places and haunt the people living in homes where the spirit once lived. There are different reasons why they return. Some spirits feel they have unfinished business. Some retain affection for their previous home and feel that the new inhabitants should not be there, so they start a pestering campaign."

C: "But why do they go into the light and back?"

G: "Because they can, just as any loving spirit has the freedom to do so."

C: "Is the place where they exist in on the other side of the veil a dark place?"

G: "Pretty much. They know that often they should not be inhabiting a person's house but on their genuine and honest request to reform, they may eventually rise up and live in a better place."

C: "So the ones that exist close to earth by choice do not have the mentality or wherewithal to make the choice to move on?"

G: "Yes and no. You see, some spirits are stuck. They believe that they cannot and will not ever be able to live in the light. For example, this is like a street person having no home to go to. He or she lives day to day in open spaces, sleeping on a bench or a shop door entrance."

C: "The difference, though, is that the homeless person may be there through no fault of his own."

G: "It's the same, except that one may have a dream, and the other does not have a dream of anything better. We will talk again on this in the future."

Negativity

G: "Negative thoughts can bring about all sorts of problems. Under the planet Saturn, there is a necessary concentration of serious effects that transpire in matter. You must not let this affect your day-to-day life to the extent that it is your whole way, if you follow me."

C: "Yes, I do, but Saturn guides my earth sign, so I feel its effects."

G: "I know you recognize that fact and occasionally put it to rights; I am not judging."

C: "I know there is always a 'but' with me. But what of the earth spirits who can cause havoc?"

G: "The old chestnut, Christine. As I have said before, pray, trust, believe, and ask for help and guidance from the archangel Michael, and then have faith."

Take the High Road

C: "You chose this subject. What would you tell me now, as some people say 'Take the high road,' and mean, 'Hit the road.'"

G: "I am using the saying to convey that when you decide to take the spiritual course of action, it will be the right one for you. The choice is guided by your highest self in conjunction with your guides, masters, and guardian angel."

C: "So, a knowing thought would drive the decision?"

G: "Yes, because your mind thinks that if it is attuned to its highest form, it will gravitate to the best way forward for you in any given circumstance."

C: "Thank you for helping me, as I am deciding whether to go it alone on a certain course of legal action. Will I win?"

G: "You have already been told that you will be in a good position, and the outcome is on your side. Save your money, and keep your own counsel. Keep on keeping on."

Calling upon Archangels

I asked this question of G over a year previous to the time of this writing. As usual, I was given a simple and straightforward answer.

C: "Is it unwise to call upon the presence and help from the ray of, say, ten archangels on a daily basis?"

G: "If you feel that you need the particular qualities of all these archangels to be with you, there is no reason not to do so. Perhaps you could consider their qualities, and then call down the resonating colour ray of the particular corresponding archangel."

C: "Some archangels work with the same colour ray, such as Michael – his is purple and gold; and Archangel Zadkiel's is purple. Do you mean that the quality of each archangel is different, even though some work with the same colour ray?"

G: "Yes, it is a lot for the human mind to digest, and so it is easier with invocation and visualisation to use the colour ray. Hope this helps. Rest, my child. It will help you recover."

Orbs and Chakras

At the time the following conversation took place, I didn't realize that I was bemoaning the fact that I had to learn the new arrangement of the archangels' sphere. This happened because the archangels in charge of our twelve chakras had been realigned. I smiled when I read back the conversation, as I was basically told to get used to working in a different way, and I should just get on with it.

C: "Are we now attuning to the twelve chakras being shown to us as coloured orbs?"

G: "Now that earth is vibrating to a fifth-dimensional level, there has indeed been a shift. Balancing your chakras will be powered with the help of the angelic realm."

C: "So, Raphael is no longer the archangel who resonates with our heart chakra?"

G: "Acceptance of the changes will embolden your energies at this moment in time."

C: "It would appear that the colour rays of the archangels have changed also. For example, Archangel Michael still resonates with the blue ray, but Archangel Zadkiel has changed to yellow and is replaced by Archangel Raphael."

G: "Ah, now you understand evolution. Surrender, accept, and move on. Your teachings can incorporate these fifth-dimensional resonations that have come about."

Finally I spoke with God on these final four subjects as I believe they will help initiates understand more fully Why we exist which I have been told by G is to bring Heaven to Earth.

Perfection

C: We seek perfection but why can we never achieve it as humans.

G: Because life on earth is a learning developmental timeline. No one person can reach perfection in the human body, again it is only part of the whole, that it has yet to reach

Suffering

C: Will you speak with me of suffering?

G: Suffering is a necessary part of the development of soul/spirit energy. An experiential part of awareness needed of the soul level to contribute to the wholeness of soul/spirit energy where it exists for eternity. As humanity continues its ascendancy more and more of its inhabitants will experience suffering as a part of the whole described. This is what I mean by wholeness of soul/spirit/mind/body that is achieved by the incarnation of human beings. Being a being is part of a whole. I do hope this is clear.

C: Very clear to me and I hope to the many who read your words.

Angels and Guides

C: A few words on this topic could help many who are just starting to seek spiritual development.

G: Ahh! Yes. Angels are my messengers of Love. Their presence brings love to surround a human with the power of the colour ray of that angel. Archangels help human beings to heal, develop, absorb spiritual knowledge, rescue, rise up to higher realms and can bring many more qualities for mankind.

C: And your Guides, Ascended Masters what would you tell us of these?

G: This you know Christine but I will talk of these to help many initiates on their lifepath. Discovering a personal guide will help a human being advance their knowledge of spirit, heavenly realms and of personal family history. Ascended Masters will inspire, uplift bring their own powerful energy and presence to advance the initiate's spiritual knowledge and need.

      As you know much more than I have just said can be gained for an incarnate on earth to help them move forward on their own lifepath, spiritually and on a soul level which is a whole other subject.

C: Thankyou for this short description which I am sure will help many take their first steps forward on their connections with their Guardian Angels, Archangels and Guides.

Will the Soul Direct Us Forward

G: This is a question most deep but I will explain: your soul will play a part that will become clear to the individual over time. This is because the soul wants you (its physical manifestation of soul/spirit) to create. Via your guide and angel the soul will seek to evolve as you develop your own physical self: meaning as you learn to follow the "higher path" i.e. (decisions made by you on earth for the good of all around you). This is not as complicated as it sounds as you well know because it can be accomplished little by little. And as your decisions become based on goodness, kindness and love so your spirit will thrive and your soul will evolve to a higher sense (resonating with love) of being. I hope these final words help you and others with more understanding.

C: Wow! that certainly is a very clear explanation, thankyou.

Blessings

Finally, I spoke with G about his son Jesus, and I could actually feel the tremendous love and emotion of his words.

Jesus

C: "Is it true what certain sources say about Jesus?"

G: "You have heard that he was not the great man history portrayed him as. This doesn't sadden me, because no man has worked with his fellow man through his heart to the degree of my son – who was God born as man – did. These naysayers only express their own opinions, getting carried away with historical figures built up to icon status."

C: "Can you name any others as an example?"

G: "Kings, queens, and religious leaders such as Gandhi and Sai Baba are but a couple."

C: "So, Jesus is fully deserving of recognition like no other before or since?"

G: "Due to reincarnation, Jesus will come and has come again, born to man, as needed by your planet. Trust, believe, and have faith. Blessings. All will be revealed."

C: "Thank you for speaking with me through my heart and mind."

G: "This is what was meant to be!"

AFFIRMATION

I forgive myself and let go of any guilt as the love of God can remove my pain and bring me peace.

Books to Read

I recommend the following books and resources, organized by category, if you wish to learn more about the topics in this book.

Souls
Journey of Souls, Michael Newton
A Seeker's Guide, Paul Williamson
Marjorie, Paul Williamson

Angels
Touched by Angels, Christine Snowdon
Angel Inspiration, Diana Cooper
Messages of Hope, Lorna Byrne
Angel Kids, Jacky Newcombe
Angel Inspiration, Diana Cooper
Archangels and Ascended Masters, Doreen Virtue
Realms of the Earth Angels, Doreen Virtue
Angel Numbers, Doreen Virtue

Psychic
After Life, John Edward
Life before Death, Colin Fry
My Psychic Stories, Jayne Wallace
Watching Over Us, James Van Praagh
Life on the Other Side, Sylvia Browne

Elementals and Angels Workshops
Alphedia's email address: www.elementalbeings.co.uk
Darren Linton's website: www.guidedbyangels.com

Planetary

The Keys to the Universe, Diana Cooper
Teachings of Silver Birch, White Eagle

God

Conversations with God, Neale Donald Walsch

We Only Know Love

We only know love
When we cry out God's name
To relieve us from suffering,
Anger, and pain.

We only know love
When the feeling is right –
When holding love's hand
Through the day and the night.

We only know love when soul touches soul.
It's granted by God
And makes us feel whole.

We only know love
When our loved one dies.
The sorrow is deep;
The core of us cries.

But love is uplifting,
And love sets us free.
It's waiting for you,
And it's waiting for me.

Sweet nectar of love,
Existing beyond earth,
Provides us with reason
For giving love birth.

White Eagle Says

The following is an excerpt from *Walking with the Angels,* quoted with kind permission from The White Eagle Publishing Trust.

Your guardian angel never leaves you. From the moment of your entering upon mortal life to the time when you leave it, and even afterwards, your guardian angel is in touch with you. It is concerned with your karma and directs your life under the control of the lords of karma. The angel is impersonal in the sense that its work is to see that you are guided towards opportunities to pay off karmic debts, or opportunities to earn good karma to add to the credit of your account. But when you do fall down and everything is chaotic, remember that there is a helper by your side. Your guardian angel has seen your fall, but will not condemn. He or she does not say, "I told you so!" Instead there is a gentle whisper within your heart, "Courage … I will help you rise again. Look up, look out! God is still in His heaven and all is well."

Praise for Christine Snowdon's Work

"Christine's story is a delightful, engaging one of hope, struggle, and fulfilment."

—Graham Jennings of *Two Worlds* magazine

"Beautiful poetry … Christine easily connects with her audience."

—Cherry Moteshar, The Oxford Editors

ABOUT THE AUTHOR

When Christine asked G if he thought her second book would be published, he gently replied, "It is my second-dearest heart's wish."

Christine is an author and a columnist with *Magna Intuitum*. She is also a spiritual angelic Reiki master, clairaudient channel, clairsentient, and clairvoyant communicator. She has worked for Russell Grant's team of psychics.

Christine's photos of angels in the sky have been published by the *Daily Mail*, the *Croydon Advertiser* newspaper, The *Sun* national newspaper, *Mu* magazine, and *Magna Intuitum* magazine.

In 2012, G (her nickname for God) told her to start using her soul name, Estrellar, for her spiritual work. This was reaffirmed in a Life between Lives session with Paul Williamson, who has been published six times and is a qualified past-life regressionist.

Since 2007, Christine's *Touched by Angels* book and website aim to raise awareness of angels, archangels, elemental beings, and ascended masters and how to communicate with them. G told Christine that combining her abilities with Reiki created a very powerful energy to work with, and her work proves this.

Over the last six years, the business became a voice for the various deities and energies through Estrellar's channellings, writings, and courses. These offer techniques to help others raise their energy vibration to become one with the planet's ascension process as it takes place.

CPSIA information can be obtained
at www.ICGtesting.com
Printed in the USA
LVHW090417020421
683296LV00016B/126